Making The Bank Wait !
How a homeowner made
the Lender wait for Foreclosure.

From

Metro Lending, Inc.
Copyright 2011
Edition 2

TABLE OF CONTENTS

Chapter 1   The Investor   5

Chapter 2   Treasure Hunting   21

Chapter 3   Moving Forward   37

Chapter 4   The Auction   44

Chapter 5   Our Day in Court   54

Chapter 6   Some Light on our Subject   60

Chapter 7   The Con Artist   69

Chapter 8   Time to Dig   76

Chapter 9   Loose ends   84

Chapter 10   Delay Delay Delay   90

Chapter 11   Get me out   97

Chapter 12   More loose ends   106

Chapter 13   Have You Seen My Note?   ...   110

Letter to the Reader

Dear Reader,

There is little doubt in my mind that what intrigued you about this book is it's title. Most likely, you or someone you know is in some sort of financial distress and were curious to know what this book was all about. You may be thinking there will be answers to important personal questions? The answer is maybe. Although I should tell you now, this book is not intended to provide the reader with a "how to" guideline in order to circumvent or avoid personal financial obligations, it is merely intended to enlighten the reader as to the rights and remedies that exist in our society and the legal system today and have been in place for many years should they be overtaken by adversity or misfortune. I would also like to take this opportunity to acknowledge to you that this book is not intended nor should it be considered legal advice. I'm not a lawyer, I've never claimed to be and I don't want to be one.

This book is written about what is widely known as the foreclosure process. This is where, for whatever reason, the borrower has defaulted on timely payments as agreed upon and the secured party, also known as the lender, is simply exercising their right to recoup the invested funds in the subject property by way of a legal action. This legal action has rules and procedures that for the most part, must be strictly adhered to and diligently so. Should the lender attempt to circumvent or alter the process, the ending result could be disastrous for the lender. A thorough understanding of this process by the homeowner could prove to be extremely advantageous as you will learn by example as told from the lender's point of view. I have been in the real estate business for many years and have experienced many of the "highs and lows" that inevitably occur through the normal business cycles. Nothing could have prepared me for the day that I, as a secured party (the lender), would be barred by court order from demanding payment or remedy from a homeowner!

This is the true story of what actually happened to me. It is written in an easy to understand format and the names have been changed for obvious reasons.

I'd like for you to know that I like to believe that when the day comes I'm laid to rest for the last time, somewhere etched on my gravestone will be this little piece of wisdom I pass on to you on which I have based most of my successes. As you take the time to fully understand and comprehend what I'm about to say and have the patience to implement it in your everyday life, your personal view of the world will slowly evolve for the better. I guarantee it and there will be opportunities galore that will initially present themselves as the contrary then evolve to your advantage and it goes like this:

"Nothing in this life is for certain and there are no absolutes, however... if there is one thing in this life that is for certain that you can bank on, is incompetence."

This book is dedicated to the loveliest, most wonderful and equally talented woman I have ever had the pleasure of acquaintance, my lovely wife. For without her, I would never have been able to sustain my sense of purpose and above all focus. Without her, sadly I must say..... I have no idea where I would be today.

Chapter 1

The Investor

I'd like to begin by sharing some background about myself and my little organization. I am a real estate investor and I buy houses, lots of them. If you've seen the billboards advertising for houses or have ever received an offer in the mail to buy your home or you've seen any of those T.V. reality shows about house flipping? That's me. Should you need to sell quickly for whatever reason, I'm the guy you would call. We try to earn a living doing what we do, and by all means, we go for a good one. Over the years, we've fine tuned our system to intentionally avoid the majority of the pitfalls of rehabbing ugly houses for money in search of profit. These kinds of projects while in theory seem almost adventurous, can take up a tremendous amount of time and money and the margin for error becomes dangerously narrow. We don't like that. What we do like are healthy and if possible, hefty profits in the shortest amount of time possible with the least amount of resistance and risk. That's how you stay alive in this business. You try to make as much money in the shortest time possible and do it consistently and quickly with the least amount of resistance and risk. This is all easier said than done especially now considering that house flipping and profits from real estate ventures are almost taboo in the wake of the sub-prime meltdown. The media and many in government would like to pin the financial meltdown of 2008 on people like me, but as many of you already know, this is far from the truth.

Success in the real estate business seems to boil down to the simplest of virtues that have been ignored by many and in some cases cast aside as folklore. Our society is riddled with the Jones' and the neighbors keeping up with them. The trick to keeping your money is not to spend it before it comes into your possession and the bigger trick to getting rich and staying rich, believe it or not, is to live below your means. This is important because it will allow you and people like me to save for a rainy day and stay afloat when everyone else is experiencing misfortune and adversity through the lack of savings and loss of income.

The ability to earn enough income through the real estate business is actually a fairly easy thing to accomplish, provided that your overhead hasn't taken the lions share of your checkbook and savings. The conundrum of the entire real estate business as an investor is to not become one of the very same people you are buying houses from that are experiencing hard and lean times.

Some of us will never understand the art and patience of frugality and most of us refuse to live in that manner until we are forced into a situation or an economic condition that is thrust upon us, which requires desperate measures and a severe adjustment in our financial well-being, whether we like it or not.

It is the American dream that any one of us here in the United States has the equal opportunity to follow our dreams and plan to provide for your family with a good life at whatever economic level that might be, and as long as that lifestyle for which you dream to enjoy is not supported by borrowing from others, may you only be limited by what you can dream and achieve.

Sometimes things happen that are beyond our control affect us in ways we never knew existed. A case in point:
When I lived in Dallas, Texas, I started buying and selling houses at the rate of 1 or 2 a month and slowly ramped up to more sales per month. I met a young and very ambitious mortgage broker who wanted to join forces with me and of course, I reluctantly agreed. Fortunately, his business model generated the leads we needed for people that were pre-qualified for mortgages and were ready to buy homes, they just needed houses. He felt that if I found and purchased homes at a discount and resold them to his clients, we stood to earn some healthy profits and it sounded appealing. After some planning and consideration, we started with a couple of transactions and all went well and my new friend and partner was easy to work with and didn't get out of hand over just a couple of transactions. He did everything he said he was going to do and I found him to be very reliable.

We turned up the volume and all was well for a few months. Then the irresistible charm of the "good life" set in and my new friend began to indulge on spending sprees. He started with a new (bigger) house, a flashy sports car and an elegant luxury car for his fiancé. I tried to bring him back down to earth and get him to understand the concept of frugality and saving for a rainy day, unfortunately without much success. As usual, one of the unwelcome drawbacks of success and money is that you draw unwanted and unwelcome attention to yourself as well as envy and animosity from those around you.

    I must say that I find it amusing that when people wish you the best and success actually does happen for you, those same people become envious and relish in your failures or misfortune. How's that for positive human nature?

    My friend the broker had created such a situation unbeknownst to me. In November of 2002, my friend had returned home from a dinner engagement with his fiancé to find a burglar in his home. The surprised burglar, out of desperation, shot and killed my friend and his fiancé in cold blood in their home and left them to die. The burglar had stolen jewelry and other wares and was dumb enough to flee in my friends' sports car. Not surprisingly, the burglar was arrested shortly after the incident. To make matters worse, the burglar who shot and killed my friend and his fiancé was none other that his own cousin.

    While this an extreme and very saddening example of envy, I only pass this on to you as an example because the threat of reality does exist. Strange things can and do happen when lots of money is involved. If you don't believe me, just read the newspaper or watch a little evening news, take your pick.

    I learned a huge lesson from what began as a very successful year to only end in a heartbreaking and a very sad year in business and tragedy. Whether I liked it not, I learned the hard way what really mattered to me in my life and certainly have never looked at material possessions the same way since.

Now back to the task at hand and the business of buying and selling houses for money. If you stay in this business long enough, in order to stay alive, there is an inevitability of evolution that will follow every successful venture and of course, many new doors open while others are left behind. What does that mean? Well, it's fairly simple, you get better at the game as time goes on and you make more money and making more money becomes easier. Sometimes though, this isn't the case and we certainly try to limit any potential losses or limits on our profits before we actually get involved. This may sound confusing or slightly off topic, so please allow me to convey to you an example.

When we first started buying and fixing houses for money, we started small with the "bread and butter" homes. These are more like starter homes for small and / or young families. Generally these homes are financed for our buyer with some sort of government loan program and/or assistance. Our average profit potential in each deal was about $20,000.00 by design. I felt this was a good number initially and it was what I referred to as safe because deals like this were fairly easy to find. Then it occurred to me one day when a deal came to me, or to be quite honest, just fell into my lap with a huge profit potential with minimal risk or rather, not any more risk than what I was already used to, so I decided to take the plunge. What the heck, I was staring at a potential $100,000.00 profit that materialized fairly quickly and without all the hassles of end-buyer financing I was accustomed to with the starter homes. So I decided that fixing one house with a profit potential of $100,000.00 was better than enduring the day to day torture of five houses of rehabs and headaches for a profit potential of $20,000.00 each. Needless to say that I evolved and adapted quickly. So I think it's safe to say that $20,000.00 paydays are great, but $100,000.00 paydays are much better, wouldn't you agree?

Now, some people call this business risky and to the naked eye, this might be so. However, these statements usually come from people that have never ventured outside of their W-2 or out on their own to earn a living without the safety-net of a steady income that a regular 9 to 5 job would provide. Don't get me wrong, there is nothing wrong with working for someone else for a steady paycheck until that is, you find yourself unemployed. In my opinion, it is never good practice to leave your destiny in the hands of another and doing it blindly. Your success or failure is to be determined by the good graces of someone else, and frankly it just plain makes me uncomfortable and I believe you should feel the same way too.

Now, to set the record straight, I don't do risky, I do risk, calculated risk. There is a huge difference. Risky is looking for profit on the roulette wheel in a gambling casino. Yes, it's possible to hit it big, however, like it or not, the odds are stacked against you. Calculated risk, involves planning and structure and more planning.

In any venture, it is detrimental to your financial health to plan for the inevitable and calculate the possibility of error and minimizing those exposures. I don't like surprises and I think it's pretty safe to assume that you probably don't either. Especially when your own money is at stake. This is the art of risk management. The planning out of the course of events that materialize and proper planning for those events that don't materialize for a multitude of reason or reasons.

In all my experience of the pleasures of lumps and bruises in this business, I've heard every lame excuse in the book about risk. Trust me when I say, nobody knows more about risk management in the house business than yours truly.

In order to effectively manage risk as it pertains to our business, all possible variables and contingencies should be taken into account before committing any measurable time and money to a project. In other words, we look at each venture with a common sense approach. We ask ourselves what's the worst that could realistically happen? If the answer is one we can live with and are properly prepared to minimize any nasty surprises, we commit our heart and soul to our work and we do so in a most expeditious manner involving a set timeline and deadlines for completion. Why? Time is money. And timing has everything to do with how well or poorly you fare in this business.

Believe it or not, it matters a great deal what time of the year you are buying and selling homes. For example, if you think you'll be able to sell a house for top dollar during the Christmas holidays, you've got another thing coming. What you've done is set yourself up for a very nervous and unpleasant holiday season. People don't buy houses during that time of year and guess what? The mortgage, escrow, title, appraisers and everyone else involved in the real estate transaction business are scarce during that time of year. They're busy doing or thinking about something else other than work. It's the holidays! People look forward to the holidays as a reprieve from the daily grind. Forget about selling, you should concentrate your efforts on buying! Most of the best discounts we've ever enjoyed when buying homes have come during this time of year. Spring and summer are the time of year when your inventory is displayed for sale. The kids are out of school and this is the time of year that most people move around.

You might, or not, be wondering how it's possible to calculate or even anticipate the unknown in this business? Well the answer is fairly simple and it comes from experience. Not necessarily yours, but it does comes from experience. I'll say it time and again, being a member of the local real estate investment clubs is a must! They will help you in ways you only dreamed of. There are many wonderful people that are ready, willing, and able to help you succeed in these organizations. Seeking them out is a very good idea. You can learn at an exponential rate by tapping into their experiences with the local market that will have a profound effect on your bottom line. So far, there are two questions to ask yourself. Are you investor minded? And, do you think this business is for you? If so, read on.

As an example, I would like to share with you an observation I've made over the course of my investing career. You see, when I was born, I seriously doubt that the moon and the stars were in perfect alignment and that I would live a charmed life. It's nice to believe in fairy tales and I firmly believe we should always be dreaming and dreaming big! Dreams are what create the world we live in. Yes, t.v, radio, microwave ovens, automobiles, the internet, cellular phones were someones dream. That someone had the conviction to see it materialize despite the contrary opinions I'm sure were floating around for the inventor. The importance of recognizing certain abilities within ourselves is imperative to either develop further in the case of a positive trait or ability, or diminish and even discard for the lack of a better description in the case of a counterproductive trait we might unfortunately possess. What does this mean?

Well, you see, throughout my investing career and most of my adult life, events or rather problems have taken place in my life that don't normally happen to other people. What this means is that I have had to find solutions to problems that don't have easy solutions. This is the story of my life. Perhaps you can identify with me on this one. I have had to learn to remain calm, thoroughly assess the situation on paper and through a careful thought process, determine the proper course of action and practice has made me pretty good at finding solutions to problems that don't normally happen to anyone else.

The wonderful part of being in this business is that we as investors are not alone. It might feel like we're the "lone ranger" out there from time to time, but we're really not. I have had the pleasure of enjoying friendships with other investors with whom we're able to bounce ideas, problems and pitfalls of the business. Generally it's referred to as a "roundtable." Investors or groups get together once or twice a month to discuss current events or the like with each other. I've always liked roundtable meetings and look forward to sitting in whenever the opportunity presents itself.

In order succeed and thrive in this business which is not a difficult thing to accomplish, I tell people I encounter or that ask me that want to begin a career in this business the same statement time and again and it's important that you hear it and understand that it exists and it goes like this:

"The real estate business is not a difficult business to grow and prosper in, but it is a business that is <u>riddled with anxiety</u>. If you don't have nerves of steel nor the ability to acquire them and the stomach for this business, do something else."

This business will constantly test your resolve. How so? One word… resistance. It comes in many forms. One of the most common forms of resistance is the delay of a rehab project for a multitude of reasons. It could be your contractor, lack of building materials, money, various municipal authorities who are interested in your project and many other fine examples. The weather certainly has plenty to do with how quickly your project moves along. Another source of resistance many people encounter but rarely speak about is the closing process of your deal when you've found a buyer and you have a purchase and sale agreement. More on this later and what to look out for and prepare in advance.

Let's assume you're fairly new to the business and have had some success. At least enough to keep you interested and on to the next deal. Let's assume you deal directly with the public or rather property owners that wish to sell. You will quickly realize that your best profits come from dealing with a specific type of seller. Let's explore them in greater detail. There are typically only three types of sellers.

* The first will sell to you, if the price is right. No sense of urgency here. This type of seller only wants to sell if the price is right.
* The second type of seller will sell to you and they want to sell, but only under certain terms or conditions and usually involving a real estate professional like a broker or realtor and most likely some form of institutional financing.
* The third type of seller "has to sell." He has to sell for some urgent reason usually involving one or more of what we refer to as the "three D's" which would be death, divorce or destitution.

This is the type of seller we concentrate most of our marketing efforts upon. Personally I prefer the latter of the D's, destitution, where a pending foreclosure is eminent or something involving financial difficulties and the utmost of urgencies are evident. Why? Usually it's because there's a deadline and external pressure upon the homeowner that has nothing to do with me. What I'm referring to is that I didn't create the "pickle" the homeowner is in. Usually it's an impending foreclosure, tax sale or the like. Whatever it is, they need money now! Generally, these sellers don't want to sell at first. Sometimes it takes a few months for them to figure out that once they get behind on mortgage payments, there is no catching up, ever. They try the usual routes first such as a mortgage company that sent them a flyer in the mail or they heard or saw an advertisement on television for refinancing or they try their local bank and maybe credit union. Usually they will apply only to find that because of the payment arrears, their credit report shows they no longer qualify for a new mortgage and /or a combination of a no equity situation.

This situation makes for added desperation and sleepless nights and of course, the prospective lender is cautious about the level of risk in this particular applicant and declines to lend. If they are able to borrow money from relatives, which I <u>never</u> recommend, the results are always the same and no matter how many times I've advised homeowners in distress against this type of loan, but they do it anyway!

The relief of foreclosure from a family loan is unfortunately almost always temporary. Eventually the homeowner ends up in foreclosure again and to top it off, they've lost the money borrowed from relatives, a rift in the family manifests itself and an estrangement between family members drives a permanent wedge between them. In the end and a year or so later after the foreclosure, the foreclosure drama is all but a distant memory but the bitterness between family members remains alive and well. This is precisely why I always advise against borrowing from family. Remember the cliché … "Blood is thicker than water and of course, never borrow money from anyone you know."
Being in a financial bind for whatever reason that eventually leads to foreclosure is bad enough, now adding the strained relationship between family members is enough to push anyone to the brink of

insanity. The homeowner then evolves into the social leper or pariah or rather, a victim, a "foreclosure victim."

We call them victims for a reason because that's exactly what they think they are when I step into the picture. They feel victimized by the entire system and rightfully so. Their job or loss thereof, the past due credit card bills, past due property taxes, past due car payments and of course the mortgage holder they are obligated to pay every month, everyone demanding payment and the constant threat of *losing it all*. It's not an easy position to endure nor would you want to be in that position, especially for an extended period of time. Some homeowners can't take the heat, some, never toughen up and evolve.

Usually when a homeowner is in dire straits, they call me. I look into their situation to see where I can help, if at all possible, and offer different solutions, but making loans to them is not an option. For the most part, when I sit down with the homeowner to make a deal, I generally end up with the keys and deed to the property and I give them some money to move. Sometimes the homeowner wants to make a deal today, then changes their mind at the last minute, especially if there is substantial equity in the property. I don't blame them, it's just that it's usually a matter of renegotiation, but it doesn't end there. With some people, renegotiation is all they are concerned with and they try to chisel you down to nothing.

Sometimes, to salvage a "great deal" we renegotiate it into a "good deal", probably not the greatest of profit margins by our standards, but it still resides within the acceptable profit margin parameters and scope of effort required for completion. So, we have to keep the homeowner under control and not let things get out of hand. If negotiations begin to get out of hand and into the realm of ridiculous, then we have to pull the plug and move on. I sort of like it when our negotiations begin to move this way because I can threaten to pull the plug early and generally the homeowner settles down and behaves himself. For the homeowner, the thought of having to find another buyer and start all over at the last minute is rarely a pleasant one.

It never ceases to amaze me that whenever we have to focus our attention on a homeowner that insists on constant renegotiation, it always comes at a time when new lucrative deals on the horizon are scarce. Hence, making a marginal deal with a fickle homeowner becomes all too important, a very poor position to be in as an investor, but it happens and should be expected.

I'd like to add a very important piece of the puzzle or rather some wisdom from the trenches at this point. This has lent a helping hand at some very turbulent times in my career, and it goes like this, " expect anything, be surprised at nothing and you'll be prepared for everything." Keeping this in mind comes in handy from time to time, but it's easier said than done. I've even thought about tattooing it on my wrist just so I don't forget.

The solution to the "fickle" homeowner came to me in an odd fashion. I was sitting in a bar, which by the way, had an entire wall behind the bar covered in beer taps that boasted brews with names I'd never heard of and from places I never knew existed. Anyway, I was having a beer with some friends, which were also in the business of buying and selling houses when they introduced me to a young man who worked for Bank of America. He started asking me questions about buying and selling loans and wanted to know if I was interested in purchasing some of their "delinquent paper." I acted like I knew what he was talking about and as it turned out, he was entrusted by the bank, with the disposition of charged-off assets. I had no idea what that meant, but I played along. You see, an organization like Bank of America, or the like, already knows that when they make certain types of loans to appease the local politicians of just about any municipality in America, they pretty much know which of those loans will sour and which, if any, will ever mature or be "paid off."

During that time, these large lending institutions were making so much money that they paid little attention to the "non-performing/delinquent" loans as they are referred to in the business of lending. These loans were to be disposed of at prices that they referred to as "salvage value." That means, they sell these loans for whatever they can get to be done with the responsibility of servicing those loans. You see, servicing a loan is bad enough. You have to send out mortgage statements, collect payments, deposit those payments, enter the data as necessary, then pay the investor who owns that loan his money and keep track of those payments etc. When a homeowner stops paying on his loan for whatever reason, the responsibility and demand for attention on this particular loan now dramatically increases and so do the costs. The Bank of Americas know this and they generally prefer to save wasted time, money and effort on these undesirable loans and just get rid of them. But to whom? What kind of person or organization would want a headache like that? Well, there are many, as long as the pricing on these loans is right and there is profit on the horizon and people like me buy them, and generally, we buy them in bulk or several at a time. But why buy them? What makes them so attractive? Allow me to explain.

  The reason we like to buy these types of loans is because it puts us in a position of authority and it's easier to keep the property owner in check and follow our game plan. I refer to this practice as "carry the big stick." A case in point:

  Remember that fickle homeowner we mentioned that insists on constant renegotiation? Well, when the previous lender owned that loan, all the homeowner/property owner really got by way of attention from the lender when he defaulted on his loan was a couple of nasty letters and maybe a phone call or two. When I become the new and proud owner of that loan, I pay a personal visit to the property owner face to face wherever possible. This method is much more effective. I make an appointment to sit down with the homeowner and discuss options and of course, his or her intentions. A day or two later, we meet and discuss usually just two options and they are as follows:
the first inquiry is to determine what the homeowner has in mind. Does he want to stay? Does he want to leave?

  If he wants to leave, generally they have no money to move. I prefer when they want to stay. This is because all I have to do is restructure his financing in a way that is beneficial to the homeowner and by all means manageable for him too. He has to be able to afford the roof over his head without taking food out of his children's mouths.

By the way, just as an observation, I always wondered why banks lend money to people at ridiculous interest rates knowing well they can barely afford to pay. Default then becomes a matter of when, not if? Why not structure the loan in a way that minimizes the risk of default and keep that homeowner in his house and current on his loan? More on this later and knowledge of the inner workings of this process can and will be beneficial to you the reader.

Now that we've determined what the homeowner has in mind, we decide on the proper course of action with the homeowner and in this case, we know he has decided to stay and wants to pay, but is behind on payments and can't catch up to reinstate.

Let's say this loan has a face value or unpaid balance of $100,000.00 and there are some payments in arrears plus some late fees and other penalties. For example, this type of loan at 10% interest, which is not uncommon, has monthly mortgage payments of approximately $1,000.00 per month plus insurance and property taxes. Let's say he's behind about ten months and with fees and penalties, he now owes about $13,000.00 and his original balance of $100,000.00. That's $113,000.00 he owes to me the new lender. I tell him that I can get him a new loan at a much better rate with a manageable interest rate, which of course I do. I'll lump in all of those nasty penalties together and start him off fresh with new lower more manageable mortgage payments. He usually agrees and I go to my trusty mortgage broker and we find the homeowner the best deal we can get even if it costs us money to buy his rate down as far as possible.

It doesn't matter that we spend real money on our homeowner and I'll tell you why in a minute. Now that we have this new loan offer for our homeowner and payments that are almost half of what they were before he defaulted, we present it to him for his approval. He's beside himself with enthusiasm and signs on the dotted line and is overjoyed to say the least. I have successfully removed the gloom and anxiety from his family life and he can now get back to normal. After the closing, I even send flowers, buy them a wonderful dinner and give him some movie passes.

With this new mortgage and restructuring, we have accomplished several things. We have saved his home, the new lender has a new loan, which is less likely to default considering his ability to pay has been greatly enhanced and this loan is now low risk for the new lender. The property taxes and insurance have been squared away, so the county offices are happy they have one less defaulting property owner to deal with and the insurance company has a good and valid policy again. The former owner of that non-performing loan has liquidated their position and of course, we get paid off at face value. This is the part I like because we paid about ten cents on the dollar for that loan or about $10,000.00, throw in a few thousand dollars for expenses here and there and we netted ourselves a health profit. Somewhere around $80,000.00. Not a bad payday! This is why we don't mind paying for this or that for the homeowner and this is why we love the non-performing loan business. We generate a healthy revenue stream with a minimal amount of leg-work. This is the essence of the business. What we do is solve problems for people and are compensated well for our efforts.

To some people, this practice might seem or appear predatory. This is far from the truth. To me it's more like a treasure hunt. There's always a story and surprises here and there. But sometimes, we encounter situations that are completely beyond what they appear to be. Obviously these are problem loans by default. Why else would the bank want to rid themselves of a headache? It's just that sometimes, being prepared isn't enough. Situations that present themselves as ordinary and with acceptable parameters can spiral out of control and leave you helpless. The story and events I'm about to convey to you actually happened to me. It is the story of how a helpless homeowner in foreclosure and about to lose his home to the bank, successfully made the bank wait for their money for over two years. He successfully convinced a judge to issue a court order against the lender to prohibit them from demanding payment. I was that lender.

I was prohibited by court order from demanding payment. This is the story of how he accomplished this. You the reader will learn how this was accomplished and how you can profit with this information.

Chapter 2

Treasure Hunting

I had been living in Dallas, Texas by design since the end of 1999 and early 2000. The real estate market there had begun to pick up speed and money was flowing and people were buying and selling homes everyday with ease. The Savings and Loan disaster of the late 80's and early 90's had all but been forgotten and I wanted to capitalize on this opportunity to transact in the business. Living in Texas and being in the real estate business has both its advantages and disadvantages. The good speaks for itself. The disadvantages generally encompass the lack of credit and money. Borrowing money is a little different in Texas than in California. In Texas, big money for real estate transactions is scarce for people like me. In California, the playing field is a little more leveled.

In California, borrowing money for a real estate transaction is much easier than in Texas. In Texas, unless you're somehow connected to the "insiders club" that run the banks and financial sector, borrowing the cheap institutional money is going to be a long-shot, unless you're part of that group, forget it mister!

Up until the late 1980's or early 1990's, there used to be a large multi-branch bank named NCNB. I don't know what those initials stood for, nor do I care, but what I do know is that many of that banks' previous executives still live and work at other banks in the Dallas metro area. A banker friend of mine once told me that NCNB actually stood for "No Cash for No Body." That company refused to make loans to anyone not on their "approved" list. I actually had the opportunity to read the summary files from the RTC (Resolution Trust Corporation) on the bank that was taken over into receivership by the government and a summary on the lending practices at the time. Many of those executives still live in the area and manage several of the smaller regional banks and continue to utilize those same old lending "parameters" established by NCNB. How they make any money and manage to churn out a living is beyond me. But I can surely say, it's not by lending. Just go to the FDIC website and look at their income statements.

Let's say that we're not part of that "in" crowd, so what's next? Well, there are always unconventional sources when it comes to raising capital. One of the easiest would be what we refer to as private money and this is where we focus our efforts for the types of projects we like. These are generally people that have some savings and for whatever reason are unhappy with the paltry interest rates they are getting on their money in a regular bank account. Sometimes these people are looking for something better, and of course, we can provide those services. For the most part, private lenders will or won't lend to you for your projects. They aren't wishy-washy about lending like their institutional counterparts are. They tend to be focused. They only want to know one thing, when do they get their money back?

Another problem I have and continue to encounter is bankers and my money. It never ceases to amaze me how people react to big money. As an example, in 1999, I sold a commercial building I had in San Diego, California that I had purchased several years prior from a bank that had foreclosed on the owner. The real estate market had improved dramatically and I decided it was time to sell. The sale was fairly quick and I was the lucky recipient of a hefty escrow check for approximately $200,000.00 that I took to my bank for deposit. I wish I had documented my visit to the bank that day.

They were sure it was drug money(an escrow check not 5 and 10 dollar bills) and I was a criminal in need of immediate prosecution and incarceration. They acted like idiots and I was furious with the whole charade. The worst part was that as time went on and the money started rolling in, the smug attitudes from the bankers never subsided. To this day, I despise going to the bank for anything and having to look at these people. Let's not forget the Post Office and the DMV. I don't care for them either! I conclude that these people are wonderful.. at something else.

A conversation I had with an attorney changed all that. Obviously I had overlooked something of critical importance, but what? The unfortunate part of being the richest guy you know is that you have no one to share thoughts with about what you are encountering, so solutions aren't easy to come by. In short, being the richest guy you know isn't good for business and not much fun either. It's very hard to grow and prosper this way. But that all changed when the attorney told me to stop using my own name for transacting business and start using company names, especially for deposits and tax purposes. No more big personal deposits to stir envy in people and I must admit that he was right. So I started using corporate and trust accounts, and guess what? The smug adverse behavior stopped. As far as they were concerned, I was just some employee making deposits for the company and no one cared. Imagine that? Still, I feel that these bankers, Postal workers and the DMV are probably great at doing something else.

      Once or maybe twice a year since moving to Dallas Texas, my wife and I pack up and go treasure hunting in California at the San Diego County Recorders Office. It's a beautiful place to visit and certainly my favorite place in the whole wide world. Say what you want about California, I've been to a lot of cities all over our beautiful country and several cities abroad, none of them come close to the beauty and cleanliness of San Diego, California! None.

      At the County Recorders office, I look for defaults, people who haven't paid on their mortgage for awhile and the lender has filed an official Notice of Default. I found a really good one, as is usually the case when you spend enough time looking. This one met and actually exceeded all my personal criteria. It was a default on a second mortgage for $500,000.00 behind a mortgage of One Million Three-Hundred Thousand dollars on a property worth, at the time, about Three and a half Million dollars. Three million dollars on a bad day.

      It's in a zip code that in 2005, Money Magazine ranked #2 most expensive zip codes in the country. I decided that there was no time to waste and made a bee line for it. I get in my car and go knock on the homeowners door to find out what's going on. Now, my wife to this day still doesn't understand why it's so easy for me to knock on someone's door to talk about their personal financial crisis. Frankly, you just get used to it after awhile. I don't care anymore and I pass no judgment. The funny thing is, in all my experience of doing this, I've found that these people are actually dying to talk to someone that will listen. Many are looking for a savior and for the most part looking for Santa Claus, something unrealistic is the norm. Some are not. You never know until you sit down with the homeowner and start asking questions.

As a rule, I only make first contact by knocking on the door, initiate some small talk with the homeowner, then make an appointment to come back a day or two later to talk. Funny thing is, this time, when I knocked on the door and identified myself and why I was there, the homeowner wanted me to come in to talk now. Hmm? I thought it was strange, but not because he wanted to talk to a potential buyer for his house, but because this guy lives in a mansion, literally. It's a giant house, he's obviously made the big time somehow, but now it's crumbling down and he wants to talk and to a total stranger? I have found that for the most part, these people have very big egos and they're very pretentious. The last thing they want is anyone to know about their troubles or that they even have troubles, much less invite you to see their world crumbling down. I've noticed that many people that live large like, this is that their life is usually built on a house of cards, like we have seen since the financial meltdown of 2008 to date. It has been unbelievable to see just how many families have been living this way that it boggles the mind.

So this homeowner invites me in and oddly, the first room we go to is the eight-car garage. It becomes apparent through our "getting to know each other" conversation that he wants me to see the two Ferraris, the Porsche, Range Rover, two Limousines, a Rolls Royce Cornice, and some other collector cars I barely remember. He goes on and on about some deal he got into with the purchase of some restaurant chain and after the purchase was concluded, the IRS came in and seized everything. It sounded real and believable, but I didn't buy it. I've dealt with IRS judgments before and all they care about is getting their money and closing the file. A question in the back of my mind asked me to verify this to be true. Would that be possible?

 What I did find peculiar was the way he reacted to me when I suggested he sell one of the Ferraris to reinstate the mortgage in question. He looked at me in horror like I'd just shot his mom.

He continued on and on about his misfortune while giving me the executive tour of his house and pointing out all the significance of every piece of tacky art strewn about the house. What it all boiled down to is that he tells me to give him Three Hundred Thousand dollars in cash and he'll hand me the deed to the house and walk away. As I was trying to process all the unanticipated events that had just taken place, I told him I had to think about it, but to give me 48 hours. I did a quick calculation in my head and it sort of went like this: If I gave him Three Hundred Thousand Dollars in cash, he still owes the first mortgage one hundred and thirty five thousand in back payments plus the one million three hundred thousand and the second for five hundred thousand plus fifty thousand in back payments. And that's all I know about so far. I still haven't even done a title search. That puts me at about two million three hundred to two million four hundred for the house. That's a lot of money to be on the hook for, I decide on the spot, no way, I just don't tell him. He smells fishy and I think something is up. I'll find out soon enough, but first things first. Let's see what the mortgage holders have to say. On the walk down the driveway to my car, I already decided I'm gonna take this one down. There's a boatload of cash in this one, just need to steer it my way, and, I need a good viable plan to sell to my wife. Without her on board for this one, I'm sunk. She's very meticulous and if I don't have a viable ironclad/watertight plan, this deal won't happen.

The next day after a very tasty breakfast in a wonderful little restaurant by the bay in San Diego, my wife and I pay a visit to the County Recorders Office. After an exhaustive attempt at researching this property and the homeowner, I concluded that this guy was in so deep, he was taking everybody near and around him down the black hole of insolvency. He owed everyone money and I mean everyone! I figured that even if I did give him three hundred thousand for the deed to the house, I couldn't possibly do anything with the house because he had so many liens and judgments clouding the title to the house, I could never convey a clear title to anyone when I went to sell.

At the time, the title report read like this:
* A Deed of Trust to secure an original indebtedness in the amount of $1,200,000
* A Deed of Trust to secure an original indebtedness in the amount of $ 500,000.00
* A pending court action for fraudulent transfer of property.
* An abstract of judgment in the amount of $ 452,485.00
* A court order for installment payments of spousal and/or child support.
* An abstract of judgment in the amount of $ 224,984.63.
* A county tax lien in the amount of $17,588.50.
* A county tax lien in the amount of $ 3,589.10
* A state tax lien in the amount of 290,203.18.
* A pending court action for forfeiture and fraud.
* A state tax lien in the amount of 12,170.80.

Up until this point, I'd never seen anything quite like this. Did it surprise me? Sort of, but not really. It was more like "par for the course." That lavish lifestyle had to be financed somehow, apparently, the easiest way was with other peoples money. It seems that everyday in the news these days, we hear of some new executive or the like being indicted or going to jail for financing his lifestyle by stealing from other people. What breaks me up is the audacity of these crooks and the gullible mentality of the people financing the whole thing. Sometimes I wish I didn't have a conscience. Maybe I could get away with ripping people off and living high on the hog.... but I can't.

So not only was this guy in hot water, he had been sued by quite a few companies and individuals and was currently in litigation with several more. But what I actually found was that this guy was ripping people off left and right. This guy was a thief. Even if I did decide to buy the house from him, the funny thing was that he didn't even own it! His son did! It was deeded to his 24 year old son. How about that? After looking closely, they have almost the same name and I suspect it was all by design. But why is the deed in his son's name? How does a twenty-four year old kid even qualify for a mortgage of a couple of million dollars? I would find out later. The way I saw it, the only way to cash in on this one was to buy one of the mortgages in first or second position at a discount and attempt to foreclose to clear the title. That was really the only way. By the looks of county records, he's got it coming anyway.

    I wanted to see who on the list of lien holders would crack first and for how much? Somebody was going to have to take a discount somewhere, it was just a matter of who and how much.

    I have to share with you at this point that my wife's eyebrows were nowhere near where they usually are. She was concerned that I'd get us into hot water just because I made up my mind to take on the challenge. I have to admit, I do get a little over zealous from time to time when the possibility of a big payday presents itself, but I never jeopardize my family or be too quick to jump. She did have a valid point about taking things slow, so I dragged my feet with our seller by showing him what I had to deal with. He had explanations for everything, just not ones that were even remotely believable. As far as signing on the deed to convey title to me, he assured me it would not be a problem with his son signing. Still, it did buy me a couple of weeks time so as to "investigate" further.

    I made an appointment to meet and speak to the first mortgage holder and they were quick to say yes to a buy-out, just not at a discount. I didn't blame them, I'd feel the same way. They were in a good position equity wise, so why budge? Our seller owed the first mortgage $1.3 million and $135,000 in back payments. But they weren't eager to foreclose. I wondered why? I mean, just because the loan in question isn't in any real danger, it didn't make sense to me to just let the homeowner enjoy the living accommodations without even attempting to make any mortgage payments. The thought of having dead money just sitting there certainly didn't appeal to me, but I guess that's the banker mentality. Sometimes, I just don't understand the logic. Normally and contrary to popular belief, the bankers generally don't want to repossess any properties. So they'll work with the homeowner to get them paying again as soon as possible and get the loan performing again. Me, I won't wait a minute. It never fails, when you give the borrower an inch, they'll want to take your arm off as you will see.

  The second mortgage holder, he was another story. As it turns out, he's the guy that sold the house to our little thief/borrower in the first place and actually built the house back in 1997. It took me a couple of days to track him down. After some sleuthing, I finally found him and paid him a visit at this home. I walked up and knocked on his door and after I introduced myself, he let me in and we talked for about an hour. I have to say at this point that it never ceases to amaze me how quickly people will open their doors to a total stranger when you come talking about money. He opened right up and wanted to sell his mortgage. Turns out, Robert Q. our thief, never made his payments to the seller as agreed. But, our seller, Walter K., was too tired and too old to really chase our guy down for the payments. To make matters worse, Walter K's lawyer wasn't helping much. His inaction's totally jeopardized Walter K.'s position and his five hundred thousand dollars plus interest. We learned that Robert Q. only made one or two payments on the first mortgage and they promptly filed a Notice of Default, which put them at an advantage. Robert Q. never paid Walter K. more than a couple of thousand dollars since the inception of the loans in question. Now Walter K. was in the hot seat to either put up another one hundred and thirty five thousand dollars ($135,000) to the first mortgage holder to protect his position, or risk the loss by foreclosure action and kiss his five hundred thousand good bye. By talking extensively with Walter K., I knew he wouldn't spend the money to protect himself, but I still wanted in.

Unfortunately, Walter K. wasn't too receptive initially and especially at a discount. I didn't blame him, he wasn't exactly in the biggest of hurries to lose money, but I knew that eventually he would come to terms with the possibility of an impending loss. As long as I stayed in touch with Walter K., I would get him sooner or later because this is the nature of the business and people. Today they usually say no, tomorrow it's a brand new day and a new opinion or point of view.

As a point of reference, I think it's important to say that at this point in the timeline, it is June of 2004. My wife and I went back to Texas to tend to business there and it would be a solid three months later that I would hear from Walter K. again. Only this time, he would be much more receptive and flexible to my requests. As far as Robert Q. was concerned, I never bothered to talk to him about buying his or rather, his son's house again. In retrospect, I should have stayed in close contact with him, at least that way, I would have been aware of his activities. But I figured that once I got my foot in the door with Walter K. and his second mortgage, I'd be in the drivers seat or rather, in a position of strength sooner or later. The only question left was how low would Walter K. go to wash his hands of the soon to be infamous or even notorious Mr. Robert Q.?

Walter K. was owed, give or take, five hundred and fifty thousand dollars ($550,000) at this point. But how low would he go? And even if he went as low as two hundred fifty thousand dollars ($250,000), and I had the money, it's just that I have a hard time laying out that kind of cash without knowing exactly when I'll get it back. It took me a long time to get here, I sure as heck wouldn't want to start over. But just in case Walter K. caved in to my offers, I needed to find an investor, someone who could put up the money, in a very safe investment mind you, earn a good solid and profitable return in a relatively short period of time? And why not? I'd done it before many times. And without going into too much detail, it took about two months of talking to unrealistic speculators to find the right investor. My new investor was willing to put up the cash in exchange for a percentage of the profits, and that was fine with me.

For clarification purposes, I'd like to share with you the options I usually offer prospective investors when I'm asking for investment funds. The first option usually involves some sort of term loan which I offer to pay attractive interest rates and usually for a term no longer than 24 months. I pay them off as soon as I can and feel it's always good business to ask for more time than actually needed. This way, when you pay off early, they are usually very delighted with me and are eager to lend to me in the future without asking too many questions. The second option involves a percentage of the profits. This method has its pros and cons. The pros usually include zero holding costs for me and I retain control of the direction of the project no matter how long it takes to fruition. The third option is one where sometimes the investor buys me out of the picture and they take over the project or sometimes the investor will want interest paid on their loan and a portion of the profits. I never agree to this method simply because we are able to find investors who are generally happy with options number one or two.

Now with cash in hand, I set my sights on Walter K. and I start calling him regularly until he's just about had enough of me. By the way, it's now mid October 2004 and it's obvious Walter K. wants out. He's had enough of Robert Q. who refuses to pay anyone, so the first mortgage holder is foreclosing and putting pressure on Walter K. and time is running out for him. He finally tells me he wants three hundred and fifty thousand dollars ($350,000) for his position. I'm impressed that he's come down this far, so I counter back with two hundred thousand dollars($200,000) just to see if he would do it and he declines. I buy more time by telling him I need more information before I can write him a check. I gave him a laundry list of documents to gather for me before I can pay him and he agrees. The only problem is that he's in the process of moving into a new house that's partially completed and his old house has sold and the new buyer wants to move in. I didn't say anything, but if his previous performance has anything to do with it, I've just bought at least two more months of fiddling before I get anywhere with Walter K. I asked him to keep me posted on his progress and let him be. I was busy with other things anyway, but the good thing was that we were moving in the right direction.

As I continued to look into what we refer to as " skeletons in the closet," sure enough, I dissect the paperwork from this particular transaction at the county level over the Internet, which is a wonderful tool by the way, and I find more questions begging to be answered. As it turns out, Walter K. doesn't own 100% or all of his mortgage. The closer I look, I find that the realtors that helped him with the sale of his mansion, still hadn't been paid their sales commissions. There were two people in the mix. Mr John, the first realtor, was still owed fifteen thousand dollars($15,000) for his part in the transaction and the second realtor, Mrs. O, was also owed Fifteen thousand dollars ($15,000) for her part or 3% interest in the note in question, which was also her part of the sale commission. This whole transaction took place in April of 2003 and they had yet to be paid. What this means is that this note had been divided into fractions, however small, and now had multiple owners.

I'd like to take this opportunity to point out to you some of the nuances of fractional ownership in mortgage notes. A mortgage note with multiple owners has it's advantages and disadvantages. The advantages of multiple ownership have absolutely nothing to do with this transaction other than spreading the actual purchase cost of the note in question over multiple investors. In other words, it's easier to sell a loan or pools of loans to a group of investors that participate together or rather "pool" their money, than trying to find just one that will write a large check for the entire portfolio. Does that make sense? Finding one investor with $500,000 or more is harder to find than five investors with $100,000 dollars each. This is an over-simplified example of how securitization in the mortgage market works. As we move along, you the reader will come to a thorough understanding of how this whole process works from top to bottom and you will see how fragile and poorly assembled the whole system really is. The disadvantages of multiple ownership in the mortgage note when attempting to foreclose on a homeowner that has encountered difficult times is that all of the "beneficial interests", meaning all the owners of that particular loan/note, have to be in agreement and concurrently act together as one to enforce the terms and conditions of the deed of trust or mortgage in question. The law in just about every state in our country requires this. Does that make sense?

    In the great state of California, under section 2924(h), it specifically states who is allowed to foreclose and who isn't by way of ownership interests. I'd like to add at this point that as far as the foreclosure laws, rules and regulations are concerned from state to state, they all have pretty much the same parameters in common. The lender must only "state" that they are the party with the authority to enforce the terms and conditions of the Mortgage or Deed of Trust in question. Unfortunately and conversely fortunately for the lender, this fact is rarely challenged in court as you will see. So back to our story

    As it appears, whomever prepared and approved the closing documents for the unsuspecting Mr. Walter K. for the sale of his home back in 2003, had no idea what it was they were doing nor aware of the consequences of their actions. Most likely, some inexperienced title attorney prepared this documentation just out of college and probably just slid by the BAR exam and is now preparing documents for everyone to sign. If you really think about it, who would question anything?.... Most people don't know any better, except of course, a guy like me looking to capitalize on what I referred to earlier as ... incompetence.

    As you recall, the original note and mortgage in favor of Walter K. from Robert Q. for Five hundred thousand dollars($500,000) had two little slivers of its face value assigned to the realtors involved in the transaction. Fifteen Thousand Dollars($15,000) a piece. A question I would normally pose at this juncture would be... "is this attorney licensed with the Securities and Exchange Commission to sell or distribute securities? After all, that's exactly what he's selling.... securities...

isn't it? When financial instruments are sliced and diced then sold to different investors, I assure you when I say that the Securities & Exchange Commission would certainly call this transaction, the sale of securities. But what I'm trying to point out to you is that these transactions can become very complex very quickly and if you're not paying attention, can become tragic and or TOXIC! So, watch out who you hire! I cannot stress this loud enough or strong enough! Unfortunately, there are far too many incompetent professionals out there that paint the picture of professionalism and it's too easy to find them.

The whole point of that original note and assignments granted, Walter K. was simply guaranteeing to the realtors they would eventually get paid. Walter K. was supposed to pay them as Robert Q. paid Walter K. from the monthly mortgage payments. But since Robert Q. never paid, the realtors never got paid either. This is where I step back into the picture and tell Walter K. about all these things I'm finding and he's impressed with my uncovering of facts. By the way, to survive in this business, a byproduct of being an investor is that you ultimately become an investigator too. I feel it's important to know as much as possible about anyone when you're dealing in big money. I use my recent findings to renegotiate with Walter K. and after a little bit of resistance, he discounts the price of the note sale another Fifty thousand dollars($50,000). That puts us at at three hundred thousand dollars($300,000). Not bad for a little bit of snooping around. But the question now is, how much better can it get and how much lower will he go?

    I'm hoping I uncover more flaws in this transaction that are fairly easy to deal with and that Walter K. has no desire to address. I stall Walter K. for another week or so to try to find other things. Unfortunately, I find nothing.

    It's November now, I'm afraid I'm going to have to make a deal soon and pay up and close this transaction or stall through the holidays. Sure enough, I get a break. Walter K. has to get back to his old country of Russia or whatever they call it now, and he won't be back until mid to late January of 2005. Perfect! I'm thinking and hoping that by the time he gets back, he'll be fed up with the whole Robert Q. thing.

As Mid January rolls around and guess what? I was right! Walter K. called me from the airport in Philadelphia to tell me he was done with Robert Q. and wanted out. So I asked him point blank, "how much?" Before he had a chance to answer, I broke the ice by telling him Two-hundred thousand dollars($200,000) today. That amount would not require me to ask for additional funding or authorization. He countered with Two-hundred and fifty thousand dollars($250,000). I nearly spilled the beans and agreed. Instead, I said I needed forty eight hours for the extra fifty thousand dollars($50,000). For two hundred thousand dollars ($200,000), he had a deal today. After an eternal deafening silence, he said OK and I about had a heart attack! He wanted to know when we could close our agreement and I told him he'd have his money as soon as I had all the documentation required. I sent him a checklist and about a week or so later, he called to let me know everything was ready.

We signed papers and he transferred ownership to me in early February when his attorney could be there to review all the documentation. It was fine with me and just part of the usual business mechanics.

My investor was impressed. Originally I had asked him for three hundred fifty thousand dollars ($350,000) and now he only had to put up two hundred thousand dollars ($200,000) plus some other incidentals. The great part was that going into this transaction, we automatically doubled the money! Robert Q. still owed us five hundred and fifty thousand dollars($550,000) and then some. My investor was happy and I was ecstatic! This was going to be a good year! I figured we were looking at a hefty payday assuming our position got paid off at five hundred and fifty thousand dollars($550,000), which meant we'd split somewhere around three hundred thousand dollars($300,000) which my part meant give or take about one hundred and fifty thousand dollars ($150,000), all without putting in any of my own dimes, or we'd get the house back in our possession one way or another and after the foreclosure auction and a clean title, we'd sell the house for somewhere around two million five hundred thousand dollars($2,500,000) or more and bank another million there! This all seemed too easy and why not? I'd done it before several times! People are people and when you can give the desperate homeowner/borrower options believe it or not, they usually help you get what you're looking for. A transaction of this size in dollar amount was certainly my first, but what I did notice was that so far the mechanics were still exactly the same as with the bread and butter homes. Better still, I was on my way and inching closer to a big payday! It was a very exciting time and things were working out just the way I thought they would.

Chapter 3
Moving Forward

I knew going into this transaction that there were some problems here and there that will have to be deal with because there always are little details loose ends. Still, it was worth the stretch. I did my best to tend to those little worms from this can I just opened which later would turn for the worst and into a heap of trouble. I already knew and have always felt, that the devil is in the details. I read it in a book somewhere, don't really remember where, but I certainly live by it. As I mentioned before, there were two people who hadn't been paid yet. So they were still in the loop and of course, I wanted them out but I had time.

After I closed the purchase with Walter K. in early February 2005, I set out to find the remaining note holders, Mr. John the first realtor and note holder, a pleasant man and reasonable. He was quick to accept seven thousand five hundred dollars($7,500) for his portion of monies owed to him to get out and wash his hands of the transaction. I prepared the documents for him to sign and I paid him accordingly and went on my way. I ran to the county and recorded my document before anything else could stand in my way. The other portion of the note owned by the cooperating realtor, Mrs. O, wasn't so easy. She was a handful and downright delusional. Her husband? Well let's just say I found him extremely amusing for the lack of a better description. This guy had a most abrasive personality of a bad used car salesman and dressed like Liberace. It took everything I had to keep my composure the first time I met him. These two peas in a proverbial pod proved to be more difficult. They were adamant about full price and wouldn't accept less than face value for their note, which was fifteen thousand dollars($15,000). They also wanted to be paid with interest even though their note had no provision for accrued interest! It made me angry that these two flakes were trying to shake me down and later I realized I overreacted to their demands and this is where I blew it. I was deadly convinced I could discount them, so I said no to their demands. And why not? Everyone else discounted their portion, why wouldn't they?

Well, this macho-man attitude I had sported at the time triggered a series of events that took me a very long time and lots of money to recover from both financially and personally. Had I sat down like a businessman and penciled out exactly how much money we were talking about at the time, which in reality was only going to be fifteen thousand dollars($15,000) and one hundred or so dollars to get them out of the picture, I would've just paid them and got them out of my life. I had failed to keep the big picture in mind and I figured that if they didn't cave in today, they would tomorrow. Why not? Everybody always does. I put them on the back-burner and felt a little time between our meetings would only serve to help persuade them into a discount for their "paper."

I thought for sure we would have to reinstate the first mortgage to the tune of $136,000 plus some other costs to protect our position and were ready to do so. We needed to get out from under that superior lien and have the Notice of Default rescinded. I felt it was a good idea to pay some prior years property taxes of about $30,000 to keep us out of tax auction with the San Diego Tax Collector. So far so good and things were going well. Our position was now dramatically improving and I felt it was time to start the foreclosure on our behalf. I was on my way to see the foreclosure company I'd used in the past for these kinds of transactions, I figured what the heck, I'd stop in and talk to Robert Q. and see what he was up to. After all, now I carried the "big stick." He had to talk to me! All I should say at this moment is that he wasn't exactly overjoyed to be indebted to me now. He wasn't shy about inviting me to leave his home, so he threw me out! Demanded I leave immediately! I found it amusing. What I was mostly concerned about was that he didn't want to talk about anything. No compromise, nothing and he still refused to pay.

I went to see the foreclosure company to get the foreclosure process started because I needed to get back to Texas and there was no need to be in San Diego any longer. It would all turn into a waiting game now and I felt I had that much. Everything was under control at this point when suddenly, I had to make some minor changes. Small details, but details that came with major consequences.

First, after I gave the foreclosure company the documentation and money to get started, then my investor had a change of heart as to how we held title on this mortgage note. Originally, it was to be held in the name of our joint venture and after some time went by, he tells me his wife didn't like that. She felt they had no control and was uncomfortable with the way their money was in a strangers hands, me. I didn't nor could I blame her and I complied with her requests to put her at ease. After all, it was their money, and I'm no thief, so I had my partner come up with a limited liability corporation and deeded his half of the mortgage to the new LLC. Mine stayed where it was. I told the foreclosure company about it, they said it didn't matter. They also said that Mrs. O didn't need to be present to sign as a beneficiary because we (my partner and I) owned 97% of the mortgage. We were the majority, so I didn't think anything of it. They know their business and the law pertaining to foreclosure, that's why we hire these people, right? As it turned out, owning 97% of the note in question was going to be an issue. I felt it in my bones. I also knew at the time that I shouldn't leave San Diego with Mrs. O and her flaky husband in the loop with important business to tend to. But I ignored my instincts.

The foreclosure company did something else I didn't particularly care for. As far as the law in California goes, the rules governing foreclosure and the documentation that's filed at the county level, you have to state the reason or reasons for the foreclosure action. Mine were as follows as is usually customary and in this order:

*Non-payment as originally agreed by the terms and conditions of the Deed of   Trust.

*Failure to pay property taxes. By this time, they were $ 42,000.

*Failure to maintain property insurance.

*Due on sale clause. Mr. Robert Q. Jr. had transferred the property to his younger brother.

I learned a couple of days later that the foreclosure company filed the documentation to read that the foreclosure was commenced because of the due on sale clause only. I was infuriated to say the least and it was now too late to correct these documents. I knew that if we went to court, there was a slim chance the judge would let us foreclose on the homeowner due to an interfamily transfer. The courts rarely side with a lender on this one, why would they side with us? Still, the damage was done and now I had to live with it. I started to have that sinking feeling. It was only mid February and we still had a few more months to go. I had to wait the full 90 days default period as required by California law and then another 30 days on top of that before we could go to auction. That meant it would be (give or take) mid June before we would see any kind of action at all. So I went home to Texas to wait it out. I was hoping this guy would refinance us out, but that was impossible, he had too many liens and judgments already at this point to be able to accomplish that. And he certainly wouldn't be able to sell the property by means of a straight sale, there was no possible way to convey clear title to a new homeowner. The only option Robert Q. had was to buy my position and foreclose on himself to clean the title assuming he wanted to? But I knew he wouldn't go for that. He had other things in mind and I knew that it would be against his pride giving me a profit. I was now the enemy, and he knew I bought this note at a discount, so naturally, he would feel he didn't have to pay face value.

So, it would be sit and wait time until June. Meanwhile, I had to get back to Texas and finish liquidating our inventory of homes. We were really top-heavy with real estate and the market was on its way down the sewer quickly, I had to move fast to get any bit of profit I could out of the inventory of homes we had before we were forced to entertain losses. I'm not a big fan of losses. We did have some good news early on in the foreclose though. Turns out that our borrower, Robert Q., thought he would be sneaky and paid the first mortgage holder $135,000 to reinstate his mortgage. The problem was that there was a discrepancy of $6,200 with the first lien holders foreclosure company. So we paid it and actually got an official reinstatement recorded at the county level. I thought that was fabulous that we didn't have to shell out any more money than necessary. Now it was only us foreclosing on Mr. Robert Q and we were in the driver's seat and first in line.

We were so busy in Texas, that June came around pretty quickly. We had sold all my inventory homes except for one, which was fine with me. We made a great chunk of change out of them and we were very happy. So my wife and I packed our bags and back to California we went. It was judgment day for Mr. Robert Q. and maybe just maybe we would enjoy another payday or at least get much closer to one? After all, there were very few foreclosure actions going on in mid 2005 and people were buying real estate any way they could! Many thought that just because there was a foreclosure auction, it automatically meant you were getting a good deal and could resell for profit afterwards. And in some cases, I guess this was true, but I was't betting on it. I was hoping someone would buy us out because I really wasn't in the mood to take on a big mortgage if we were successful in foreclosing on Mr. Robert Q. But I kept my fingers crossed anyway.

I'd like to add and point out to you that the ownership of our Note and Deed of Trust in question now had three owners. Our company, my investors new LLC and Mrs. O. The California rules governing ownership or beneficial interests in Note and Deeds of Trust, when a foreclosure company is hired to perform the duties of the "Trustee" and will be referred to from here on as the "Trustee." All beneficial interests acting in concert to enforce the terms and conditions of the Deed of Trust, need all to sign on the dotted line of the paperwork governing and hiring the Trustee. If one of the beneficial interests has not authorized the action, you don't have a valid foreclosure.

Just so you know, most states have rules that govern these processes and investigating these processes

by way of subpoena and discovery, prove to be
extremely effective in delaying the foreclosure process.

Chapter 4
The Auction

In the great State of California, the "drop-dead date" is five days before the auction. That means, a borrower has until five days prior to the date set for auction to make up any back payments owed to the lender, and the lender, no matter how much he despises the borrower, has to take the money, then the loan is reinstated, the Default is rescinded and the process starts all over. Get it? The loan is now current. This is where my concerns really began and I like to share with you as to why.

I'm about to explain to you what is going on out in the world as we know it today concerning mortgages. This is something I found while researching public records during the normal course of my business. When I relayed my findings to a couple of the high profile Real Estate Education Gurus that I know personally, they didn't believe me. In fact, the only people that believed me were my wife and a few close associates.
It was then that I realized that these guys , "the gurus," are more concerned with selling books and tapes, and I don't blame them, we all need to make sales and that they were not keeping up with the new trends. Or maybe, I thought to myself, maybe these guys just talk a good talk, but have never actually been in the trenches. My wife has asked me repeatedly to join them on the Circuit, and while tempting, I like my life the way it is with my wife.

The trend I stumbled upon is what I call, for the lack of a better description, "One Payment a Year" and this is how it works. If you don't believe me, I'll be happy to take the Pepsi challenge with you any day of the week and prove it to you. No lender will ever admit that this is or has happened to them because it exposes some of the flaws in the system, especially when you want to sell some of these types of "non-performing or sub-performing" loans to someone else.

The borrower, first has to find himself in default before he realizes he has latitude within the system. Then he learns quickly and adapts. He then becomes or rather evolves into what I refer to as, the "Foreclosure Victim", and finds himself in the midst of a foreclosure action. We call it, "Once in Foreclosure, Always in Foreclosure." And you best watch out for them.

I have included several media examples for you to peruse and verify.

The borrower, for whatever reason stops making his mortgage payments and we'll use California Law for this example. (It is no different anywhere else in the country, the process changes a little here and there, but the basics are always pretty much the same). Ok, you're in California, let's say, the last payment you made was January, lets keep it simple. February comes, you don't pay. So what? You get a late fee, big deal. March goes by and you still don't pay, you get another late fee, maybe a letter or a phone call or two, but that's it. April goes by and the lender might just send you some hate mail and another late notice. This is usually the case, depending on how many loans they have in inventory already souring. It's very rare a lender will file a default on you, the borrower, after just 90 days of no payments received. If they do and you challenge them in court, chances are the court will side with the borrower and not the lender. The lender tends to look a little over zealous or even predatory if they are quick to jump the gun. You let May go by. The lender will want to work a deal with you. Some kind of deal and unfortunately, most suckers fall for the forbearance plan, which means you make payments higher than the normal amount until you get caught up with the past due payments. This plan has never made sense to me because if the borrower couldn't pay before, how could you pay now at an even higher rate or payment schedule?

So let's say you go for the forbearance plan. This is very common. Your payments, for example, are supposed to be $1,000 per month. You are behind four months or $4,000. The lender says if you send us $2,000, we'll work with you on the rest. Now, its important for you to know that all this communication with the lender is very cumbersome and time consuming. You can easily squeeze another 30 to 45 days or more depending on whether holidays interfere. But for this example, let's say they don't. We're at the end of May early June. The lender gets tired of you. They threaten to begin foreclosure. You say and do nothing, you just ignore them. Two or three weeks later, now it's mid to late July, they file a default. From the default filing, the lender must wait 90 days before he can take you to trustee sale or auction. So that puts you into late October or early November before they can post your house for auction sale which will be conducted no sooner than three weeks or 21 days later. Now you are in late November early December. You owe approximately $11,000 to $13,000 in back payments. Seven days before the auction, you make up all those back payments with fees and other stuff added. The lender must accept it by law and by law they must reinstate you! Now you have been reinstated and you can start the process all over again in January hence "One Payment a Year program." This is what is going on out there. I can't tell you how many lenders have tried to pawn their chronic problems onto me with this exact same scenario lurking in the shadows. This could be considered one way to beat the lender at foreclosure and it is only the beginning.

    Now back to Robert Q. and the auction. My wife and I got back to California about a week prior to the foreclosure auction. The foreclosure company, or rather, the Trustee, says they haven't heard anything from our borrower, but a lot of people have called to find out about the sale. That made me feel good to know that someone might bid this sucker at the auction and get us out. Then it happens. Some lawyer, whom the Trustee knows from prior dealings, shows up to their place of business. He is representing the borrower, Robert Q., and has a subpoena in hand and wants copies of everything and is challenging the foreclosure process. The Trustee tells me not to worry about this "Po-dunk" attorney as they called him. They had beaten him before, as she so brazenly and eloquently stated to me with conviction. I took a moment to formulate my response to her. I told her with conviction not to underestimate anyone! I told them that I personally know a "Po-dunk" Texas attorney that peeled 150 million dollars from FEMA for some farmer in Oklahoma. He did it all pro-bono and didn't let up. So don't underestimate him. She didn't say anything more. I knew we were in trouble because there were just too many little glitches with this action and I was rightfully concerned. Sure enough, the next day, three days prior to auction, I get a summons for a hearing on a Temporary Restraining Order, or a TRO as they are referred to in the court system. I didn't understand this one. I thought TRO's were used for domestic disturbances and such. Generally a borrower files for bankruptcy protection to stay the sale, and that is expected. I've dealt with them before and while they do cause a delay in the auction, it's really no big deal. It just takes an additional 30 to 60 days to have the stay lifted. But the lender always wins or rather, it's rare that the lender loses.

So now I have to answer to this "TRO" and I asked the Trustee to recommend an attorney and they give me one, a Real Estate attorney by the name of David L. and I go talk to him. He didn't understand why the attorney filed for a TRO either. I should've followed my instincts again and walked out the door right then. He would prove to do more damage to my case than I could possibly recover from. I just didn't know it yet. Use of the "TRO method" has since become customary in fighting foreclosure actions in San Diego County. This is the first weapon used against the lender to pull the lender into the legal arena and delay the foreclosure process these days.

In the beginning, Robert Q., through his attorney, pleaded with me to grant him 30 days to either pay us off or at least reinstate his loan to the tune of about $170,000. I didn't want either. But I caved into my attorney's advice and granted 30 days because he felt that the judge might frown upon us, the greedy lender, and grant the TRO and preliminary injunction. I wanted to take my chances in court and I suspected David L. was just too chicken to challenge it. He wasn't about to come out and admit it to me, but what I do know he wanted was the money. After some deliberation, I said OK to 30 days. What the heck, it was only 30 days and if I was going to be stuck somewhere for 30 days, there are worse places than San Diego California that's for sure! What I didn't know and I doubt David L. knew either, is that TRO's are almost always granted and have a life of

21 days before a hearing is set for a Preliminary Injunction, which means that they're trying to get you to stop doing something or prevent you from doing something. David L. never told me any of this and probably because he himself didn't know. Some Lawyer!

    You remember when I said before that things that happen to me don't really happen to anyone else? Well, just so happens, this was to be the first of a wave of TRO's as an alternative to Bankruptcy stays in San Diego county. It figures! I'd be at the front of the line on this one and have to figure it all out without having a model for comparison. To this day as you are aware, foreclosures have mounted exponentially from 10-20 per month to several hundred per month and getting worse. To my amusement, sort of like a personal joke, TRO's are filed every month against lender's trying to foreclose every month on about 70% of the foreclosure filings. Most of them are granted. Hearings for Preliminary Injunctions now clog the court calendars. If you're a lender and want a speedy hearing, good luck! The court calendars are so backed up, it'll be 2-3 months just for a Preliminary Injunction hearing. If the judge finds anything amiss with your loan or foreclosure, anything at all, he'll set you up with an Injunction hearing, and set trail. Did you catch that? Trial, for a foreclosure? And trial will most likely be at least a year away. That means your borrower stays where he's at without having to fork out a dime to the lender, he just has to feed the lawyer. It will more than likely be cheaper than paying on the mortgage and property taxes and so forth. How do I know this? I've found that judges tend to find something, even if it doesn't exist and they reluctantly want to evict some poor homeowner out into the street. Trust me when I say, he'll find something.

    So now I have to wait 30 days and I'll just grin and bear it, but deep down inside, I knew it was a mistake and I've still got one loose end, Mrs. O.

    I started trying to contact them to pay them off, but they avoid me like the plague. I decided to be the tough guy, and pay her another visit at her office unannounced and of course, she's not there, but her husband is. I show up on my Harley dressed in leathers and park by the front windows where the whole office staff can see me drive up and I can't help notice the whole office is staring at me and probably wondering what's going on. He comes out, looks around at everybody and quickly escorts me into their conference room. It had the desired effect and we negotiate for their little $15,000 dollar interest in my note. After going back and forth for an hour, I decide to just cave in and give them their money, all of it. As far as I and the law was concerned, all the paperwork on this foreclosure action led us to the fact that Mr.s O and I were partners, like it or not. If I went all the way and foreclosed on Robert Q., now she would have an interest in the property and not just Fifteen thousand dollars worth anymore($15,000). She would have to sign off on anything we wanted to do with the house just like a business partner would. This was not a position I wanted to be in and if I had just taken care of this six months ago, we wouldn't be scrambling. It was bad news and I had to get her out as soon as possible before matters went from bad to worse!

    After going back and forth, we decide on $15,000 dollars in cash in a day or two. They insisted on consulting with their attorney and I agreed, but they wouldn't tell me who their attorney was. The fact of the matter was, they didn't have one. It was just a smokescreen to buy some time.

    Two days went by before I started making calls and of course, they make themselves scarce, again! I already had the check and paperwork for them and finally we talk and agree on a time to meet. The whole thing was like pulling teeth and dealing with children and just plain ridiculous. I quickly start making my way over to meet them and get stuck in traffic, and all of a sudden it hits me. A little birdie tells me to call them and of course, as is predicted, Mrs. O and her husband tell me they already sold their interest to somebody else? Somebody else? Are you kidding me? Good grief? And to top it off, they won't tell me to whom.

    What a joke! I was furious! Not so much at them, they were just stupid and playing some childish little game, no I was furious at myself for allowing these things to get out of hand when I could have so easily taken care of the loose ends before they became urgent matters like this!.

I had already suspected to whom this "interest in the property" would appeal to. I mean think about it, it doesn't take a genius to figure it out, who else? Obviously someone with a vested interest in making it very difficult for me to move forward on my foreclosure action. I also suspected that whomever they sold it to, would run to the county offices to record their interest, I just had to wait a couple of days for it to show up. There would be no way they would buy or acquire this interest and not protect themselves by not recording and sure enough, that little 3% or $15,000 dollar interest shows up at the county office and it's registered to a guy with the same last name as our borrower. I couldn't believe it! Are you kidding me? They couldn't pick somebody else? How arrogant and ignorant? Maybe a company name? A trust? Anything but someone with the same last name as the borrower being foreclosed on. It's now only obvious to anyone interested that the borrower is stalling the foreclosure in ways that show intent on refusal to pay as agreed on the Deed of Trust. I ran to our attorney.

David L. and he tells me this is great because it shows the court bad faith on the part of our borrower. He felt that the judge would see this and rule in our favor and allow the foreclosure to continue without further delay. I felt the same way and found myself in better spirits now that it seemed our ship was steering in the right direction, so we waited anxiously for our so called, "day in court." I honestly felt we had our borrower beat and we were getting closer to our much anticipated payday. And why not? His side of the equation was looking pretty bleak. I figured that as long as our attorney was able to present to the court the following, the judge would be hard pressed to deny our petition for dissolution:

*First, for almost two years, the borrower hasn't paid on the mortgage in question.

*Second, he hadn't paid the property taxes either and owed more than $50,000 dollars to the county in unpaid property taxes.

*Third, they refused to pay and maintain the required homeowners insurance.

*Fourth, they hadn't paid the homeowners Association dues either and the association had now filed a lien against the property.

*Fifth, the title to the property had been transferred to someone else without the lenders consent triggering the "due on sale" clause.

*Sixth, the title to the property was now impaired with all kinds of liens and judgments!

I mean, this guy owed money to all kinds of people. All of these factors were direct breaches in the mortgage contract. I felt it was a slam dunk and pretty difficult to argue? I felt there was no way this guy could get out of having to pay us either with money or the property. I and our attorney were confident this charade would stop immediately! One thing about foreclosure I knew up until that time without a shadow of a doubt, is that one way or another, the lender always wins! Always! Don't believe me? Stop paying your mortgage and see first hand what happens.

To me, this guy was just another loser who didn't want to pay his bills. It wasn't because he couldn't, it was because he refused to! Simple as that. I didn't feel too sorry for him, especially after the conversation I had with him about selling the Ferrari to make his mortgage payments. Too many times, I'd encountered people like him living far beyond their means and in the end, it always catches up. The part that always breaks me up is that they honestly feel they are the victim and there's always a story of some tragic and unforeseen circumstances that mystically appeared.

When I first got really going in this business, I bought the stories and I honestly did everything I could

to try and help, but I quickly realized there are always, three sides to any story:
What he said, what she said, and what really happened.

Our day in Court was just a couple of days away and victory was eminent.

I'd to take a moment to point out to you, the reader that finding glitches in material facts about the lender in question, attempting to foreclose on a borrower is not a difficult thing to do at all. Homeowners in distress should first look at ownership of the Deed of Trust in question, because if there are multiple owners of that note, it's going to be pretty hard for the lender to enforce the terms of the Deed of Trust. If there are multiple beneficiaries, especially as is the case where many loans were issued and sold as securities in pools to be sold on Wall Street, including where MERS(as nominee) or Mortgage Electronic Registration System is concerned. More to follow later in this book on their function and why they exist will be explained to you in later chapters. Multiple ownership or beneficiaries in mortgage notes is dangerous and potentially disastrous for the lenders that engage in the business of buying and selling cash-flows as they are referred to in the industry. Most of the processes that include the structuring of securities in order to sell pools of loans to investors in bulk have been circumvented and title been destroyed. As you are going to see, we are only beginning to scratch the surface of the tip of the iceberg as to how to make the bank wait, in perpetuity, for their money.

Chapter 5
Our Day in Court

The 30 days I granted as a grace period to our borrower was finally over. We encountered no attempt to refinance, no attempt to reinstate or negotiate some sort of settlement, nothing. The little trick our borrower used, with the 3% interest in my note, was amusing my team to the point of hysteria. Everybody was positive our borrower would be thrown out of court and out of his house very soon, and not just because he didn't want to pay, we all felt he just plain deserved it!

It just so happened, a friend of our "Trustee" had been burned by our borrower for about half a million ($500,000 dollars). It was something having to do with a restaurant and I really didn't pay too much attention to the case or what it was about. They had a judgment against our borrower and a lien on the property. But since it was farther down the line of title from us, I didn't really care, but I should have paid closer attention.

I have to admit to you at this point, that I was really concerned with the abilities of our legal counsel. To say the very least, I was not impressed with David L. I had to educate him in matters where I felt he should already have solid understanding. After all, this was a real estate transaction, and he was, or rather, called himself a Real Estate attorney, and I was stuck with him. The hearing coming up was only a hearing for a temporary restraining order, certainly not rocket science. By this time, we're in mid July of 2005 and I go to the hearing and sit in the courtroom until they finally call our case. The attorney and the judge all stand up and walk out of the courtroom. I'm wondering what the heck was going on? Ten minutes later, David L. comes back, nonchalantly, he tells me the judge granted the restraining order. I was dumbfounded!

Outside the courtroom, I demanded to know everything! First question, why did everybody walk out of the courtroom? David L. tells me that this hearing is what's called an "ex parte" hearing. It's like an official hearing, but not. Now he tells me? I'm furious to say the least! He tells me the judge granted this TRO pending a hearing for a preliminary injunction, about 30 days or so later. He said the judge felt there was cause to grant the motion. My second question to David L. referred to his presentation. I asked if he presented everything? He told me the judge didn't care. We would sort it all out in the next hearing in 30 days or so. We would get our money a little later than sooner, but I was not convinced. Still, I had no choice but to grin and bear and ride it out. I tried telling myself over and over that this is how it goes for the big money. I tried to convince myself to just be patient and it probably would have worked if there weren't so many little problems with our foreclosure action. I felt the clouds begin to move in and the uncertain and sinking feeling was now very real and right in front of me.

    I really didn't know what else to do and unfortunately, I was in uncharted territory. All I had were my wits and inadequate counsel to rely upon to get me closer to my payday. I was beginning to get worried. I was getting a good stiff dose of the realities of the legal system. It doesn't matter what or who's right or wrong, all that matters is who knows the system better, and, as I would find, who's connected, who isn't and who knows. It was obvious, that our attorney, was clearly not in the "click" at the courthouse.

    The Trustee I hired, were confident that we would get our way at the preliminary injunction hearing. They felt that since our borrower was such a crook and because of all the liens and judgments on the property, even if the judge ruled in the borrowers favor, the borrower would be required to post a bond for the benefit of the lender as financial protection equal to the amount in question, which was about $600,000 dollars at the time. But no bonding company would ever do such a thing considering there were so may liens and judgments against the property and the borrower could not be trusted. They kept telling me not to worry. Don't worry, huh? Famous last words!

    Our attorney David L. was in rare form. He started coming up with all kinds of stupid suggestions on how we should settle. Settle? Settle on what? We have a borrower that refuses to pay his mortgage and obviously everyone else. It's not he's just having a bad year, he's clearly in the business of stealing from unsuspecting people. But settle? I couldn't believe it. Instead of acting on the offensive like I wanted him to, this guy wanted me to throw in the towel. What he was really telling me was that either he was out gunned, or too old to put up a fight for his client and just plain too ignorant to know what to do. Either way, it was time to get rid of him and I knew it was really time to get away from him when his daughter, the secretary, felt the need to tell me about her past cocaine addictions and bisexuality. It just all cracked me up and I couldn't believe what was happening. These people were a joke, and they were making a joke out of my business. Of course, the one thing they were good at was their hands out for prompt payment, that, they were good at. I was becoming angry, and angrier by the minute.

Our next hearing would determine the proper course of action and about a week before our hearing, I got an envelope with Robert Q. pleadings they filed with the court. Apparently, their biggest argument was the fact that we refused to allow our borrower to reinstate his loan? So, I called our Trustee to see if she had received a copy of the same package. By this time, our borrower owed us about $130,000 dollars. In this package, was a copy of a cashiers check for $115,000 dollars payable to our company via the "Trustee." It represented an amount which the borrower claims to have tendered to me, the lender, and apparently, I or someone at my company refused the payment. I think it's important to provide some definitions for your understanding. The word "tender" as used in this context, means to present for payment. I never got such an offer, but Robert Q's attorney was adamant and claimed to the court that they did in fact so tender the check. David L. was indifferent and felt I should have taken it. I could've strangled him! I never even saw the check until Robert Q's attorney filed a copy of it with the court. Clearly this was misrepresentation and our attorney seemed to be siding with the borrower. He didn't hear a word I said. The hearing was just a couple of days away, and he was obviously not prepared. I knew it and of course, he did ask for more money.

The next day, David L. types up all the documentation to submit to the court saying how we oppose all the allegations and how we should be allowed to collect our money, etc. etc. I didn't like how it was written it, but still I had to play along. I figured, we would get somewhere after I found out that most TRO's are granted anyway, but it's the next hearing where you get to present your case and the judge makes a decision, right?

Wrong! How wrong? I was about to find out.

It's now mid August 2005 and we're sort of ready to go to court and put a stop to this foolishness. Clearly the borrowers attorney is a fraud and I carefully read all his pleadings and letters and not many of them made much sense. They were poorly drafted, and left material facts out, he was also clearly fabricating the facts. I thought for sure he would be caught and the court would penalize him.

David L. our attorney, was better prepared and in much better shape than the borrowers attorney, Luther L. but unfortunately that doesn't say much about either one, considering I felt our counsel was an idiot. Oh, don't get me wrong, he liked to talk tough, he just wasn't too bright and bore little common sense. The day of our hearing is at hand and I walk into the courtroom and I see that our Trustee is also there, she was also curious about the outcome. The court clerk calls our case number and we're up.

David L. stands up for us and introduces himself to the judge. The judge cuts him off mid-sentence and calls out our borrowers name and says, "how much has this person paid on this mortgage? $500,000 dollars? Isn't that enough?" I'm horrified to say the least and David L. did nothing to correct the judge. Then the judge asks for the opposition, Luther L. to state his case and did so in the absolutely worst way possible. Let me tell you, he sounded so pathetic and spoke in a crackly little voice and clearly scared to death. His oral argument had nothing to do with the case at all and I was sure David L. would beat him with our points of the case against the borrower. Instead, the judge ordered a Preliminary Injunction just like that! He didn't want to hear anything from David L. and to make matters worse, David L. didn't even put up a fight! I was already boiling mad when David L. meekly asked the judge for a bond to cover us, but he sounded like a scared little girl, a far cry from Mr. Tough guy, and the judge said no. David L. didn't even tell the judge that the law says its mandatory, not optional! I just got spanked down again and it would be months before we could get on the court calendar again for the second stage, an injunction hearing. I was speechless. I went home and drank myself into a coma. David L. had nothing to say, nothing to add, not even a suggestion as to what now? It was time to get rid of him and unfortunately, I was now prohibited by court order from moving forward in the foreclosure in anyway whatsoever. So what now?

     As you can see, it isn't difficult to delay the lender with simple arguments, but you will need the assistance of and even mediocre attorney. As is happening in todays society with the fall of the real estate market in most of the country, many people choose to stay in their homes until the foreclosure by the bank is complete and then off they go. Sometimes they even stay until after the outcome of the eviction hearing. Should a homeowner decide to put up a fight and stay in their home as long as possible. As a business decision, you might find that it is much cheaper to pay an attorney $8,000 to $10,000 to run interference for you for an indefinite period of time than pay the lender. As you will see, anything is possible if you have the guts to stick with the program and fight. Just keep in mind, the object of the game is to make the bank wait, for as long as possible.

Chapter 6
Some Light on our Subject

So what now? Where do we go from here? Instead of answers, all I got was more questions. The first question to answer was, "where do I find a great attorney?"

Obviously a mediocre one was not going to be acceptable. They only serve to do more damage than good when dealing in actual court appearances. Unfortunately, finding a great attorney is literally like finding a needle in a haystack, it is not an easy task. But perhaps looking for a specific professional isn't necessarily the object in mind, we just need someone that will do what we ask and keep the mistakes and errors to a minimum.

But whom? A couple of days later, I got a copy of the judges signed order. I had to read it a few times to thoroughly understand the order and each time I read it only served to infuriate me more and more. The order read as follows:

Pending the hearing of this order to show cause and motion for preliminary injunction and until further court order, the Defendants, their agents, officers, employees and representatives and all persons acting in concert or participating with them (Restrained Persons) are restrained and enjoined from in any way whatsoever proceeding with the Trustee's sale of the subject property. The Restrained Persons shall cease all foreclosure activity under said Notice of Default and said Notices of Trustee's Sale pending the preliminary hearing as set forth.

I sat in my car in the parking lot for awhile contemplating my predicament, and it dawned on me that no one here except me was playing by the rules, so I figured, why should I continue to do so? I mean, what are we trying to accomplish here? We've got some jackass trying to get out of paying his mortgage, and he's succeeding! It's not like I'm trying to rob the guy, I'm just trying to collect on a debt he signed up for long before I got here. I'm just trying to collect what I'm legally entitled to.

The order prevented me from any action against the borrower, but what if I sold or transferred the subject note to someone else? Theoretically, they could move forward? After all, the order did not prevent me from selling or transferring of the note in any way shape or form. I figured, what if I created a new Trust or entity and put my wife as the managing Trustee to handle all the affairs of this "new" Trust. Why not? Nobody had ever seen my wife, and we would use her maiden name for all documents. I would become her employee or consultant to see things through? Frankly, I thought it was brilliant! Well, sort of. But by doing this, I figured I could put the ball "back in play," so to speak. It was theory after all, I really hadn't thought it through but hey, what was the worst that could happen? Nothing or I'd end up right back to square one and at a standstill. Still I had to do something, I couldn't just sit here waiting.

    I went home and sat down with my trusty computer and got to work manufacturing a whole new entity. Documents, checking accounts, licenses, business cards, etc.

Still, I needed a new attorney and preferably one that understands what I'm doing and trying to accomplish. But where? I decided it was time to find out more about our borrower. I felt it was imperative to know who exactly we were dealing with. So I went to the courthouse and started pulling files from all those people who had and were still suing our borrower. But there were so many files!

    I couldn't believe my eyes. There were so many cases involving our borrower, it took me days to sift through everything. I got tired of reading them all. After all, they all said the same thing. He borrowed money from many people and didn't, couldn't or wouldn't pay it back.

    As a sidebar I'd like to add at this point if I may, I remember when I first started in this business, one of my biggest fears was being pulled into litigation or being sued for the lack of a better description and I can tell you with certainty that being in the real estate business invites litigation. It's not a matter of "if" you'll get sued, it's "when!"

The common denominator to all the files I had poured over was that our borrower was either a con-artist and/or a thief, and very successful one at that! I began to understand how he was able to talk people into lending him large sums of money. He definitely had a good story and a great show! He lived in a very big house, drove expensive cars, dressed impeccably well and appeared to want you to share in the astonishment of successful ventures. He even had a huge picture of himself that was taken with the then President of The United States. It hung in the foyer under accent lighting and beautifully framed he was very proud of. That same picture was also imprinted on the back of his business cards. I thought it was an ingenious move. I wondered if he was actually affiliated somehow? But I guess that was the whole point? If you were the lucky recipient of one of those business cards, what would you think?

I did find out later, through the grapevine, that Robert Q. had contributed $30,000 to the Republican Party for that picture when they were in San Diego a few years back. Apparently, that was cheap compared to what it did for him. Obviously, it served him well and sort of made him look well connected and even successful. Another thing I was learning about our borrower was that besides being no stranger to litigation, this guy knew the law and legal system. There was one file in particular that got my attention that really opened my eyes to how devious our borrower really was. I found it's contents extremely insightful and amusing as well. This story is taken from actual court documents filed and it went like this.

      Robert Q., our borrower, went into business with Raymond G. Raymond G. was a very wealthy, prominent, respected and now retired attorney. He also owned a very popular upscale restaurant in San Diego. Somehow, Robert Q. talks his way into becoming partners with Raymond G. in the restaurant business in order to streamline operations and of course, expand! So naturally in the course of business, Robert Q. asks Raymond G. for a loan of $100,000 dollars for reasons undisclosed in the file documents. Robert Q. promises to pay it back in fifteen weeks with $15,000 dollars in interest and of course Mr. Raymond G. goes for it and advances funds. Once the fifteen weeks are up, Robert Q. repays Raymond G. back all his money with the promised interest and everyone, especially Raymond G. is happy.

A few weeks later, Robert Q. goes back to Raymond G. for another loan for reasons undisclosed in the file documents but this time requests $200,000 dollars. Of course Robert Q. promises to pay it back in fifteen weeks with $30,000 dollars in interest and the eager Raymond G. goes for it and advances funds. After the allotted time passes, Robert Q. repays the loan at the time promised and just about 30 days later, Robert Q. returns to Raymond G. and requests a loan for $300,000 dollars. But this time, Robert Q. entices the lender with a promise of $60,000 dollars in interest in fifteen weeks and of course, Raymond G. goes for it and advances funds for the endeavor.

When the allotted fifteen weeks are up, Robert Q. is due to repay to Mr. Raymond G. his $300,000 plus the promised interest but unfortunately, is a no show. When Raymond G. starts making inquiries as to Robert Q's whereabouts, Robert Q. dodges for awhile only to infuriate Raymond G. further and demands the return of his money. Robert Q. simply says that he doesn't have it and to not bother him anymore. Raymond G. is furious and threatens to sue for the money but Robert Q. is faster on the draw by slapping Raymond G. with a lawsuit claiming usury! He sues Raymond G. for usury. If you don't already know, usury means charging an interest rate higher than normal rates and in this case, the interest rate on that first $100,000 would be approximately 52% interest calculated on an annual basis, terms obviously slightly higher than normal interest rates at the time.

Now considering Raymond G. was a licensed attorney fluent in matters legal, he realizes that just about any judge would probably show little mercy on him and instead, a settlement agreement was drafted between Robert Q. and Raymond G. out of court which of course, our Robert Q. never honored nor did he intend to. Raymond G. got swindled and he knew it and the worst part was that there was little he could actually do about the whole mess. Robert Q. never repaid Raymond G. a dime and managed to get away with $300,000 dollars of Raymond G.'s money. I thought it was devious, cruel and brilliant all in one. I also realized that I had found my new attorney with an axe to grind against our Robert Q., the borrower in question.

This is how I met Kevin R. He was representing Raymond G. against our borrower Robert Q. and I'd spoken a few times with Raymond G. about Robert Q. and the whole fiasco. He recommended Kevin R. for several reasons and most of them relating to his abilities as a attorney and litigator. So, I made an appointment to speak with him and ask several pointed questions to put me at ease.

During this time, I had completed our "new entity" and transferred the "note" in question and funded the new Trust. I had intentionally established the new "Trust" outside the borders of the State of California to make it more difficult for the opposing party to "serve" us with any papers. I also needed to make it look like a legitimate transaction. I felt it was all very important for appearances sake.

I had consulted with our Trustee and their counsel and they felt I was correct in my assumptions about the "Ownership" change and how that pesky "Restraining Order" didn't apply to the new owner. I never let anyone know nor were they even the wiser as to what was going on with the new changes. All they knew and figured was that I sold my "interest" because I was broke and needed the money. I'd like to add at this point that I find it amusing at how easy it is to keep people from prying into your affairs, just tell them you're stone broke and you might hint at needing to borrow some money to get by. Trust me when I say, they don't ask many questions after that!

Matters were certainly shaken when all the new notices were sent out to all interested parties about the scheduled foreclosure auction on our borrower. We all figured that since the new owner of the "note" in question wasn't prohibited from continuing to foreclose on our borrower, we'd move things along.

What happened next proved to me how "rinky-dink" the civil legal process is and can be. A borrower can easily capitalize on its weaknesses with even the basic knowledge of its workings. Luther L., our borrowers attorney, had objected to the foreclosure posting and since we were doing this foreclosure posting from outside the State of California, it would be impossible for him to serve us with any summons all by design.

    For those who don't already know, before you can get in to see a judge, all parties to the lawsuit must be served first. This is how the process starts. Our friend Luther L. served the Trust at our former attorney's office, even though David L. wasn't representing the trust. The part that infuriated me and served to make me more suspicious of the whole process, was that the court accepted this service process as valid. I couldn't believe it! So, again, Luther L. was successful in obtaining another "TRO" against the new Trust, the owner of the "note" in question. We ended up dead in the water for a couple of months after that, again. Well, I figured it was worth a shot.

    It was during this time, that my attention to a junior lien holder was directed. Our borrower, had swindled a Chinese couple out of $600,000 dollars and they were not amused and they certainly didn't give up easily on our borrower. They stayed on him to pay until our borrower agreed to give the Chinese couple some collateral on the money Robert Q. took from them. Robert Q. had signed a mortgage on the house giving the Chinese couple security for their loan. Well, what Robert Q. didn't count on, was that the chinese couple would attempt to foreclose on Robert Q. to get their money. I received notice of this sale and promptly made an appointment to speak with them. The Chinese couple were extremely welcoming people and I sat down and spoke with them about our mutual acquaintance. As it turns out, they knew a whole lot more about our borrower than I did. It seems that Robert Q. already had some history and I found out he had already been imprisoned in the early 90's for swindling people out of money. He had served four years in a Federal Penitentiary in Oregon for fraud. The Chinese couple suggested I speak with their attorney and they said I could get everything I needed from him. There was one thing for sure I found out, that they did not want to foreclose on our borrower Robert Q., but they did want to sell their position, and, they wouldn't accept less than full price on their note. I thought to myself that it was a price I was certainly not willing to pay. I tried to work out some compromise where I could takeover the mechanics of foreclosing on they're behalf so they could get their money. Eventually I would then get possession of the property and clean it up then sell it off. The only problem I had with that scenario was that now I had to make sure there was an extra $600,000 in profit just to pay them off. I wasn't crazy about it, but at the time, I had no other viable options. In the end, they wouldn't work with me and I never heard from nor spoke to them again.

    I was very anxious to know more about our borrower, so I ran to their attorney's office, Jack M. He was not as receptive as I anticipated. In fact, he was arrogant to the point of ignorant and downright insulting. He didn't want to hear anything about anything. But he did give me some good information about our borrower and the real business he was in.

    Again, as you can see, delaying the inevitable is as easy as baking apple pie, you just have to stick to the program! Staving off an impatient lender isn't as difficult as one may think. I'd like to add at this point that research is imperative! I cannot stress this point enough. Two very important points commonly overlooked when mortgages are transferred between beneficial interests(ownership) are county records and the Secretary of State's Office. Four questions should be answered when an eager lender is attempting a foreclosure action on a vigilant homeowner. They are as follows:

    *Who-   is foreclosing?
    *What-   documentation do they have to prove beneficial interest(ownership)?
    *When-   is the foreclosure action scheduled and when did this lender come into
    possession of this loan?

*Where- is the beneficial interest located? (state? country?)

You will see the importance of research in the coming chapters and many questions will be answered for you. Never lose sight of the fact that the object of the game is to delay for as long as possible. As time goes on, a very important factor which you will come to rely on will become your ally, incompetence! Use it to your advantage and do not allow yourself to be victimized by it.

Chapter 7
The Con Artist

In all the years I've been in the real estate business, nothing had prepared me for what I was about to discover and encounter with Robert Q. I've run across a few derelicts and delinquents in the past. Petty thieves here and there and some shady characters. But now I had officially encountered a professional con-artist and convicted criminal and I had the proof. I had a full copy of his arrest and conviction record along with his incarceration order. The file had all kinds of information. Apparently, at one time he was the subject of an ongoing criminal investigation. In the larger multiple page report written by the FBI agent that arrested Robert Q., it talked about Robert Q's restaurant business, or rather what the FBI agent referred to as: Roberts' "bust-out" business. I had in my hands, the entire explanation on how he operated on paper and neatly typed.

But before we get into our story further, I'd like to share with you some information about some of the mechanics of the sale of a restaurant business. This information will help you gain a more logical understanding as to the business affairs of our borrower and where he fits in, so to speak and what he does.

As you may or may not already know, the restaurant business is a tricky high-risk business. Most of the independents fail within the first five years of operation which is usually due to undercapitalization and of course, poor management. As a restaurant owner, your odds of survival are greatly increased *if* you have a good location. But a good location costs money, so we're back to capital limitations. The burning question for every restaurant owner is, do you have the money to weather the ups and downs of the business? Well let's assume you do and we'll fast-forward a little. As you would probably guess, owning and operating a successful restaurant business is incredibly time consuming. You will be there 24 hours a day, seven days a week no matter what! Let's say you've been at it for a long time, ten, fifteen, maybe twenty years or more and you've become a staple in the community, everyone knows you and how to find you. Your restaurant is perfectly located, well capitalized, low debt and a great money maker. The day comes that you decide you want to retire and either do something else or just retire and go fishing. So you put the restaurant up for sale. Eventually, after receiving an offer or two, you will realize that in order to sell your restaurant for cash, there are certain concessions you will have to make whether you like it or not. First, you'll realize and eventually come to grips with, is that there is virtually no institutional financing for restaurants. In other words, if I wanted to buy your restaurant, I can't just go to the bank and borrow the money to give to you so I can take over ownership, management and make mortgage payments to the bank like I would for a house or a car. On the other hand, all cash buyers for your restaurant are going to be far and few between and you can bet that anyone who shows up with cash will most likely demand plenty of discounts and concessions. To make matters worse, you'll then have to accept the fact that you are eventually going to have to help with the financing, whether you like it or not. What does that mean?

We're referring to seller assisted financing. Remember, you want to retire, right? Well, assuming you find a buyer, and that buyer has some sort of credible down payment to give you and for the remainder of the balance, you are willing to accept payments over a period of time. But now, who will you sell to? I seriously doubt you will sell to someone who doesn't know the first thing about restaurants or the business and it would be unwise to do so. The only way you will eventually sell is to someone you're obviously conformable with. You'll want to make sure you'll get the remainder of your money. Right? Also, receiving payments over time isn't so bad, as long as they don't stop coming in. You'll be able to go about your retirement or new plans in no time and everyone is happy. This concludes the background lesson on seller financing.

To get back to our story, this is where Robert Q. comes in. He looks for you, he finds you, he meets with you and you like him. Let's take this scenario a step further about your success. Let's say you own not just one successful restaurant, but several well located restaurants. They've been around for awhile, probably a staple in the community. And here comes Robert Q. He's charming, dresses well, drives a real nice car, knows the business lingo, has the big house for you to see, oh, and he'll hand you one of his business cards with his picture of the President and himself printed on the back for you to see. When you visit with him at his house as his guest, he'll show you around, maybe you'll stay the weekend, probably takes you for a ride in one of the Ferraris and most likely, you get to drive! Impressed with his success yet?

So now, you get down to brass tacks with Robert Q. and talk business.
For examples sake, let's say you want one million dollars for your restaurants. He'll agree that the price is reasonable. He says something to the effect that he'll give you $200,000 dollars or so right now as a down-payment if he can make payments to you over a period of time and agree on terms for the balance. In the back of your mind, you've already accepted the possibility of this method of sale and of course, he'll reason with you and say it's necessary because he needs time to take over the new restaurants, bring in personnel, etc., etc. Of course, you agree. After all, it's all true and necessary and besides, he's handing you $200,000 dollars in cash. That's a respectable down payment and certainly nothing to sneeze at is it?

Now you go see his lawyer, you probably bring yours along. Robert Q. will tell you that all the credit accounts need to stay where they are for now until they can open new ones to replace yours as the transition begins to take form. You sign on the dotted line and probably go on vacation with the first class tickets he's purchased for you! Then Robert Q. moves in and get to work.

He immediately starts running up all your available credit lines and all the withholding for the employees payroll taxes are withheld by Robert Q. to be donated to his favorite charity, his. He keeps paying the employees to keep them working and they don't have any idea that those taxes aren't being paid on their behalf. He skims as much cash as he can from the businesses. He might even make several payments to you to keep you happy and out of his hair. Months later, when he stops making payments to you, you'll complain. When you complain loud enough, after all kinds of excuses from him, he'll throw you a bone. Some cash to keep you happy and out of his business. Eventually, all the debt, and new credit lines he's run up on your behalf becomes so great that you find out one way or another. In a fit of rage, you confront him and after long drawn out excuse and explanations, he apologizes to you throw his hands up in mock despair. He probably admits to you that this time, his luck just wasn't there.

After signing everything back to you, he'll take off leaving you with the wreckage and aftermath to deal with. You'll probably want to sue and recover monies from him once you have a full accounting of the damage he has inflicted on your behalf. You speak to your attorney and decide a lawsuit is probably the best course of action and you go ahead and file. Robert Q. barely puts up a fight and you think this will be a slam dunk. He doesn't even show up for court to defend himself and you get what's called a Default Judgment for all monies you asked the court to grant you and guess what, the judge throws in a little extra for you. You think you won and for all intents and purposes, you did and you go and celebrate. Finally, a ray of hope through a very dismal time-consuming process that has your nerves in shambles! But guess what? When your attorney refers you to a collection agency to collect on your judgment. You will eventually find that there are no bank accounts to tap, no property to seize and no Robert Q. anywhere in sight. He's probably siphoned an incredible amount of money from you over and above the $200,000 dollars he gave you and you have no choice but to file for bankruptcy to clear all those debts from your name. This entire process, believe it or not has a name and is known as a "bust-out." Mr. Robert Q. is known by the FBI as a "bust out artist."

Maybe in the end, you'll find him and his whereabouts and you're so upset, you try to turn him into some law enforcement agency. You know what they'll say? They say that most of their resources are devoted to violent crimes and yours is a civil matter. Sorry, we can't help you. At that point, you will realize that Robert Q. just got away with all your money and then some and there is nothing you can do about it, and worse, he knows it!

As of this writing, I have personally verified Robert Q. to have taken an excess of Fifty Million dollars from unsuspecting restaurant owners in Hawaii, California, Arizona, Oregon, and Washington. He is good! The best I've definitely ever seen, and to tell you the truth, I actually kind of respect him for his audacity. He has destroyed countless lives and livelihoods, toppled countless restaurants and several restaurant chains you might be familiar with if you live in those states all without conscience or remorse. The FBI prosecuted Robert Q. in the early 1990's but not because of all the "bust-outs" he had been involved with. It was because he lied on a couple of loan applications he made to a federally insured institution back in the late eighties. It just so happens, those loans went bad and the FDIC had to reimburse the lender so it became a "federal" matter. They, the government, didn't care about the "restaurant business", they focused their attention on the loan application. That's it! Amazing isn't it? They threw the book at him and got the maximum penalty which was four years incarceration. If Robert Q. hadn't tried to defend himself and hired the services of an attorney, he would have got away scott free or at least with a much more lenient punishment. Instead he went up for four years all for lying on a loan application.

When I first uncovered his motive and direction, I was so floored and horrified, that I became bound and determined to not be another one of his victims. The good part about my position is that I had a secured position in a high value property. I wasn't going to let up for one bit At least now I was well aware of who I was dealing with and what he was capable of. I knew now to expect anything and be surprised at nothing!

So what have we learned in this chapter?

Well I think that it is imperative to hire counsel where necessary for matters you may or may not fully understand. I also believe that it's imperative to protect yourself from the ravages of unscrupulous people or organizations, as is evident by simply tuning into the evening news. Every day we get news reports about how this or that has taken place and if someone had only done this or that, the whole calamity could've been avoided.

But how does this apply to you the reader? Well I think we should all stay on our toes and keep a watchful eye. As the current economic meltdown persists, many more injustices will manifest themselves and as the level of desperation increases, so will the crimes committed upon the unsuspecting public.

Chapter 8
Time To Dig

Our new found information about our borrower made me paranoid for several reasons. First, we obviously weren't dealing with your run-of-the-mill petty thief or wise guy. This guy was a professional and quite successful to boot. He also had resources that money can buy like lawyers to keep the wolves at bay from all directions.

All of the files on Robert Q's endeavors I read at the courthouse included high-profile prominent attorneys or law firms. He definitely had the money to hire the best counsel which is what concerned me the most because, of his current choice in counsel, Luther L. I asked myself, why would Robert Q. hire some no name attorney, out of his own neighborhood, to handle a delicate subject like the foreclosure of his home, his pride and joy? He obviously knew something I didn't, and the burning question was, was this attorney somehow connected at the courthouse? Friends in high places maybe? Or did Robert Q. have the connections and it didn't matter who represented him? He could pick the last slug on the attorney welfare line and he would always get his way no matter what? I guess it was the paranoia setting in. What didn't help me was that in the headlines of the local news of the day, was corruption in the San Diego courts. Apparently, San Diego County is no stranger to corruption in the court system. I guess there's been so much hank-panky with favors for this or that if judges rule this way or that way and so on.

Perhaps I was naive, but it just didn't make sense to me to go through all this for a simple foreclosure. I felt that Robert Q. should just pay up or get out and move along! To me, he was just another worm trying to weasel out of paying his bills. On the other hand, even if there was corruption in the courts I was staring into, I would still have the daunting task of having to prove it with concrete evidence, which is no easy task. But how?

Robert Q. had done prison time in Oregon and I felt we were lacking some vital information about him. Unfortunately, at the time, the state of Portland Oregon's County Office system was in the electronic dark ages when it comes to records research. The Internet was not going to help me here at all and I figured I would have to go there personally to pull files. So my wife and I packed up our bags and the car and off to Portland, Oregon we went. A day or two later we got to Portland Oregon, a beautiful city, but unfortunately for my taste, it rains way too much!

    I didn't find much in Portland records, but what I did find was interesting. Robert Q. was using his sons name Robert Q. Jr. to mix-match names and social security numbers on various documents for intentional confusion. It was through a search of old records I was able to determine who's signature belonged to whom. You see, Robert Q. would claim identity fraud or "sorry you have the wrong guy" in just about every document, credit application and lawsuit he was trying to circumvent. The part that amazed me was how easily he would confuse everyone and also just how easy it was to get away with it.

    I also found that Robert Q. Jr. was following in his fathers footsteps. He had been picked up by the Portland police for shoplifting from a department store. He paid a fine and got a a little probation and was quickly gone. Another thing I found in Portland were several judgments against Robert Q. from Hawaii. It seemed he owed a lot of money out there, just how much, I didn't know so I told my wife that I felt it was a good idea if I went to Hawaii alone to investigate Robert Q. some more. She didn't go for it. But I tried. All in all, I didn't find much by way of profound significant earth-shattering documentation on Robert Q. in Portland and the trip was almost disappointing. I worked quickly and got out of there. What it did give me was clearer insight on who Robert Q. was before and after prison. What I found was that he was much smarter and faster when he got out of prison. I had heard in the past that if you wanted to learn all about white-collar crimes and the how to's, go to any federal penitentiary and ask the prisoners. Who better to learn from than the pros? Some people even call it crime school and for good reason. Unfortunately, I was also learning more than I cared to learn and I was starting to see that I was being misdirected by the legal system. You see for them, everything is about details and like the old lawyer's proverb, "the Devil is in the details," I knew that if I didn't cut Robert Q. off at the pass, he was going to run all over me. It was on the drive back to San Diego from Portland, that I decided that the only way to fight fire was with fire. I was bound and determined to find out as much as possible about our borrower that I could, and maybe use that information to stir up a hornets nest.

My first stop was going to be with the FBI. After all, they had already prosecuted him before? Maybe they'd get him again? It made sense to me and I had proof. One thing for sure, I was going to complain to anyone who would listen because I figured that eventually some of these skeletons would come back to visit Robert Q's closet. If I could get enough of them together to get his attention, Robert Q. would know what I was up to and maybe, just maybe, he would want to call a truce and pay me off. It was a long shot, but it was all I had.

Back in San Diego, I went to the courthouse and started pulling records on our Robert Q. again. Unfortunately, in one of the files I had overlooked the first time, was all that information I got from the lawyer Jack M. Had I looked at it closer and not just disregarded it like I did before, I would've learned sooner who our borrower was.

I personally went and interviewed everyone that would talk to me who had either sued or was in the process of suing Robert Q. I asked a lot of questions and gave away a whole lot of information in hopes of making things easier for the victims and much more difficult for our borrower. I figured that if he was going to rake me over the coals, I was going to take him with me. The more the merrier!
Unfortunately for the victims, all the information I gave them didn't help one bit. And the multiple visits to the FBI? Well, I'll just say that the agent assigned to this investigation that interviewed me and would do so a few times later, was, for the lack of a better description, clueless. I was so disappointed. This is what happens when you've seen too many of those cops and robber movies to make me think law enforcement like FBI

actually cared and had boundless resources and maybe they do, just not for Robert Q.

I even went to see the San Diego Economic Crimes Division. I gave them an entire book of how Robert Q. operates and all those people he had taken. You know what their response was? The detective told me this guy was too complicated for their resources. They didn't have the manpower for something like that. They are too busy prosecuting hot-check writers. The Sheriffs office didn't care either. The Attorney General? They were a joke. Every law enforcement office I went to was indifferent. They didn't care. One police officer actually said in his own words that nobody cares if some rich person gets ripped-off. He said they probably deserved it anyway. I was floored. Nobody cared! I was starting to see clearer now that Robert Q. knew exactly how law enforcement would react. He was way ahead of me and I was drowning in despair. This guy definitely knew the whole system and how to get away with it all. I kept asking myself how I was going to take him down? Our court date was coming up soon and I was hoping I could get him picked up by the cops. That way, maybe we could use all this information against Robert Q. for our day in court. Anything!

I also figured it was a good idea to send copies of all the documentation and history I had on Robert Q. to his attorney. I figured that maybe it would put a psychological cramp in the defense of his client. I don't think it worked, but I had to try and I still had one problem to be solved, Robert Q. had assigned that little 3% interest in my note to a relative by the name of Alex Q. I still had yet to find him and I needed that 3% out of the way, but where was he?

For all the scams Robert Q. ran and the audacity in which he conducted himself, he did have a flaw that I noticed early. Robert Q. was very good at talking people out of money and probably better at manipulating people. Actually, good is not an accurate description. In my opinion, he was certainly the best I'd ever seen or encountered. And emotions aside, I respected him, but he still had a vital flaw. The reason so many people were able to sue him and take him to court and get judgments, was because Robert Q. did business in his own name. This was the kiss of death for Robert Q. and he also fell apart when it came to the paperwork. Robert Q. left a trail like a snail, and that was his downfall. In actually, it was because of his paper trail that I was able to find out so much about him. If he had knowledge of working with trusts and limited liability corporations and simple shell companies, no one would ever know he existed. Especially law enforcement.

    Robert Q. knew all the workings of the legal process and I mean every step! What I'm referring to is the actual workings of the system, And if I may, I'll give you an example as it was presented to me. Let's take a quick look at the service process. When you sue or are being sued, everyone involved must be officially served. What this means is you're putting the opposing party on notice that an action is moving against them for whatever reason. The process server then signs an official statement that process was in fact served upon that person. That official statement of the service process goes in the file at the courthouse, then there is a deadline to file all pertinent documentation with the court clerk before your hearing in front of a judge. Usually, the deadline to accept paperwork pertinent to your file is about two weeks prior to your hearing. The file will make its way to the judges office about a week before the hearing by the court clerk. So let's say, there's one week prior to look at the file before going to its department. One week after the deadline to file all pertinent paperwork. Anyone can view the complete file at the courthouse. But remember, no more paperwork will be accepted to that file after the deadline and before the hearing. When you request it, the file is pulled for your viewing. Generally, the clerks that handle these files are indifferent or are concerned with matters rarely involving work. They're just your average everyday Joe's and Jan's trying to earn a living and aren't too concerned with the health and welfare of your files. Don't believe me? Go and see for yourself. So, anyway, if the file is viewed by an interested party, and while the clerks are unaware, seemingly innocent but critical documentation is removed, like the service process paperwork. Eventually, when your hearing is called up and the lawyer contests the service process, the judge looks at the file and has to agree and throws the case out for lack of service. The judge then calls up the next case and yours is over and out just like that! It's that easy! You will then have to reschedule and pay fees again and it'll be months before you're back on the docket. Does this information amuse you? It didn't amuse me when I became victim to these shenanigans. This is but only one minor example of knowing the mechanics of the system, the true and actual mechanics. You could have hired or even be a brilliant attorney, but if you or your brilliant attorney don't have a firm grasp and understanding of the actual mechanics of the system, you will lose every time to those who do. You can bank on it!

    This is where I went to speak and hire Kevin R. and from the moment I met Kevin R., I knew we were in qualified hands. I don't have much respect for lawyers, probably because of the ones I've encountered, but Kevin R. was very good at his profession. He was very down to earth, however, expensive. Fortunately for us, he was already familiar with our borrower and his character. I felt this would help our cause and also, our borrower had already beat Kevin R. once before with Raymond G., so I felt there was an axe to grind. Kevin R. felt he could get things back on track with my case and drew up all the necessary documents to file with the court and set us up for a hearing in mid-November 2005.

    What I was very concerned with was that Luther L., our borrowers attorney, was gaining on us. He had filed a TRO and managed to successfully enjoin, meaning mix together, the old lawsuit with my company and the "new" Trust, (the owner of the mortgage in question). The judge actually went for it, and felt it was just me trying to get around the system, which was true, but I kept my mouth shut. Kevin R. tried to have us separated but the judge said no and Kevin R. thought it was odd, and he told me that the maneuver of selling the note was a good move, but the court wasn't amused with this tactic.

    Now, I believe it's important to say at this point that I understand why Kevin R. took my case, but I'm very disappointed in him for a fundamental reason which was because he didn't fight the initial service process which I felt held a tremendous advantage for us. Luther L. had served the "new" owner of the mortgage in question at our previous lawyer's office. David L. had written to Luther L. stating he did not represent the new "Trust" and Kevin R. ignored this flaw and I felt he did so because he wanted the money and ultimately cost us over $50,000 dollars in legal fees. That part, I'm still sore about. But back to the task at hand.

Every time I spoke or met with our attorney Kevin R. about Robert Q. and his career, he was floored. He couldn't believe that Robert Q. was walking around out there ripping people off and no-one had more positive action to limit his wrath. I had to agree.

What have we learned in this chapter?

Well, I believe in knowing your opponent well and never underestimate them or their counsel. I believe intimate knowledge of the mechanics of any system not just the legal system is a must! We should pay strict attention to the smallest of details that could be skewed to our advantage and capitalize upon them. I believe this goes without saying and above all, never rely upon anyone, especially government agencies, to jump to your cause or rescue. As is evident, derailing the foreclosure process isn't exactly fraught with obstacles. As you will come to see, making the bank wait for their money, literally can be all fun and games! The question is, are you willing to play to win?

Chapter 9
Loose Ends

Unfortunately, the court would still not let us set foot into the courtroom until we could prove we owned 100% of the mortgage note in question. Can you believe that? These days, the banks can't prove they own *any* notes they are foreclosing on unsuspecting homeowners. But, I can't foreclosure on a borrower who hasn't paid in over two years and clearly refuses to pay anything. The issue of that little 3% interest in our note that used to belong to the realtor, Mrs. O. and sold her interest to someone related to Robert Q. Here is yet but another example where Robert Q. was able to make the bank wait even longer.

In this case, Robert Q., while extremely savvy, falls apart with the details. He had assigned that 3% interest in our note to someone bearing the same last name and even the same mailing address. Not very bright at all! He should have just filed it into his own name which would have made it impossible for me to foreclose. In my opinion, at least he should have used someone else's name, or a corporation, or even better, a trust of some kind. Had he done this, it would have been impossible for me to find this mystery relative.. Our attorney, Kevin R. felt it was imperative we have this 3% out of the way. With it out of the way, there would be no more argument in court about this little technicality and the obstacle it presented.

I kept being a pest with law enforcement to get them involved and still, they could care less. The victims I spoke with seemed to think that some how they were immune to the wrath of Robert Q. and I felt it was more denial with these people than anything else. They actually thought they would recover their money, despite the fact that I told them who Robert Q. was and how he operated and still, I couldn't seem to get anywhere. I even turned him into the I.R.S. I filed one of those whistle-blower forms you hear about with the I.R.S.

I used to believe all the bull you see and hear on TV and the newspapers about how you don't mess with the I.R.S. I'll tell you right now, those stories you hear about are isolated cases. The investigator I spoke with felt this case wasn't worthy of their attention, even though he owed millions in taxes and fines. He felt it was too complicated. Too complicated? I had just handed him months of investigation, I had it all mapped out! I handed it to them on a silver platter and they passed! What a joke! He was apologetic, that he was. He told me they only go after the weak average Joe that doesn't know any better, Robert Q. already knew the game. The investigator told me that even if they could indict him for tax evasion, it would be years before they would get him into court. All he had to do was hide behind his lawyer, which he was certainly entitled to, but by then, Robert Q. would be long gone. I was so disappointed on one hand and amused on the other. This was interesting information. So I made note of it and filed it away for future reference. You never know...

Robert Q. and his sons by this time had managed to purchase a few more restaurants in California from some unsuspecting sellers. Two in Palm Springs, two in Laguna Beach, one in Modesto and another in Stockton. I took the liberty of sending these unsuspecting sellers a complete profile of Robert Q. I never heard anything back from any of them except one. If you can believe this, they felt that since they had an attorney, they would be immune. Apparently, these people didn't fully read my package.

Our attorney Kevin R. with my unrelenting help, was able to serve Robert Q. Jr. with a summons for a deposition. Just in case you don't know what that is, it's just a process where the opposing attorney wants to ask you or the opposing side a bunch of questions. What happens is, you show up for the deposition with your attorney to answer some questions, but guess what? You don't have to open your mouth and say anything but, "I don't remember or I don't know." You think this is a joke? I did. I was under the impression that somehow later in the process, this deposition would make some sort of difference with our case in the future but guess what? It didn't, at all. It was just another way for the lawyers to siphon more fees and trust me when I say, that's it! I sat in on the deposition on Robert Q. Jr. and it was nothing but a circus, but I did get one little piece of information out of the whole fiasco. Robert Q. Jr's employer and the whereabouts of this distant relative

Alex Q., the holder of the 3% note in question. I did a search online and I found him in Las Vegas, Nevada. I did an extensive profile on our mystery guest and as it turns out, his whole occupation was identity fraud. This guy had so many aliases, it wasn't even funny. I wonder how many lives he destroyed? But the reason I found him, was because he had filed for bankruptcy in Las Vegas, Nevada. What I didn't understand, was why he would do that for a measly Five Thousand dollars on some medical bill? I knew I'd find out later.

While Robert Q. Jr. was enjoying his deposition, I went out to see what kind of car he drove. It was a Suburban with Arizona plates and I took a picture of it with my phone and gave it to our attorney. Our attorney later asked for him to produce his divers license, but Robert Q. Jr.'s attorney, Luther L., told him not to present it. I couldn't believe it. Kevin R. asked for his social security number and still nothing. When Luther L. demanded to know why, Kevin R. gave him a copy of an IRS tax lien I found in Arizona against Robert Q. Jr. for 1.5 million dollars. The look on Robert Q. Jr. and Luther L.'s face was priceless. I had found this tax lien through my investigating of these people and I know they were surprised at my ability to find out anything about anyone at anytime.

After Robert Q. Jr. calmed down, because apparently he didn't know that he owed the I.R.S. 1.5 million dollars. This 24 years old kid, already on the hook to the government for a ton of taxes, he blurted out the name of the company he worked for and of course I ran with it. A few days later, I would find out about the new restaurants. What I also found out, was how the system for obtaining liquor licenses in California works. I'm not gonna go into a lot of detail here, but I will say that if you want a liquor license in California, just buy an existing one. You could have a criminal record 30 pages long, and nobody will care. They will if you apply for a new license!

It was at this time I found out that the corporation owned by our borrower, was suspended by the California Franchise Tax Board for non payment of state income taxes. They owed about $785,000 in back taxes and when you don't pay your taxes, California will suspend your corporation and theoretically, you can't do business in California. Notice I said, theoretically. If nobody complains, nobody cares, but I called and I complained. My complaint was all about how Robert Q. had at the time, six restaurants he had just bought and was applying for the transfer on the liquor licenses.

I filed these complaints with the Alcoholic Beverage Control based on the issuing of liquor licenses to a suspended corporation. They seemed indifferent, but it definitely worked. The ABC gave Robert Q. just a couple of days to pay his taxes and reinstate his corporation to the tune of about $785,000. Ironically, this amount was almost identical to the amount he owed me. If he hadn't felt my presence before, he sure felt it now. At this point in his game, he couldn't afford to get his liquor licenses yanked. I told our attorney, Kevin R., what I had done to Robert Q. and he thought it was hysterical. He couldn't stop laughing. He said it was the best joke he'd heard in a long time and he laughed so hard, he couldn't stop coughing. I thought he was gonna keel over on the spot.

I contacted the bankruptcy Trustee for the bankruptcy court in Las Vegas. I told him everything I knew about Alex Q. and his family and he was very interested. I gave him my entire file on these people and as it turns out, just a couple of days later, Alex Q. would have a hearing on his bankruptcy case and since Alex Q. had stated no assets in his case, he could be in big trouble for lying on his bankruptcy petition. Obviously, he had assets, well, at least one, this 3% interest in the note in question worth $15,000. His bankruptcy petition was only for $5,000. The Trustee confronted Alex Q. about his petition and other identities and gave him the opportunity to file an amended version.
I thought it was great that evil people were getting what they deserved.

The trustee told me I could buy the note from the court, so again my wife and I packed up and headed out to Las Vegas for the weekend. I had to be there the next morning or there was going to be difficulty on the purchase later on. So I drove all night to be there bright and early and I met with the Trustee in the morning. He had a whole lot of questions for me and he also wanted to know if I would help prosecute this guy. Help? Of course I would help! I was already thinking courtroom drama and all expenses paid trips to Las Vegas for testimony, etc. But, all he needed from me was the okay to pass on the information to the Department of Justice and a sworn statement. That's was it. How disappointing!

I attended Alex Q's hearing and was pleased to hear his petition was denied. The court was happy to take my $15,000 and give me the documents that now showed I was the legal owner of that miserable little 3%. I was ecstatic! On the way out of the courtroom, Alex Q. bumped me with his shoulder and gave me an evil look so I stopped him outside. In my best mafia look and tone, I told him to tell Robert Q., his cousin, that the games were over and if he didn't pay me, I wouldn't stop until he was back in prison. I also told him to thank his cousin for the criminal charges he was now facing. I'm not sure it really worked, but it made me felt better. It was just one of those things. The tables were turning for the better, and I felt we got a little closer to getting paid. For the moment, my wife and I relished in this little victory and enjoyed the rest of our weekend in Las Vegas. My wife hit a Royal Flush on a video poker machine for $1,200 dollars and it paid for our trip. I called our attorney Kevin R. and he was ecstatic. He couldn't believe I actually accomplished the impossible. I had found the proverbial needle in the haystack. So I got the gold star for the day!

Chapter 10
Delay Delay Delay

It's now mid January of 2006 and the last hearing we scheduled for October 15th was a failure, no, it was a joke. The judge we had, opened his argument by stating he had already ruled on this case and was not going to change his mind. Kevin R. our attorney, was floored and I think it was at this point that he started to believe me and my paranoia about Robert Q. and his possible influence in the courts. This judge wouldn't even let anyone speak and as predicted, dismissed the case. The only choice we had was to file for a change in judges and Kevin R. agreed with me all the way. But, we had to wait, again, for the new judge to be assigned by the court clerk and then have a hearing scheduled. I wasn't exactly jumping up and down for joy about waiting until late February, a little over a month later and as you can imagine, all of this delay is extremely frustrating.

By this time, my nerves were worn so thin, it was starting to take its toll on my personal life. My wife couldn't believe how things were going either. I had begun to tell my friends and relatives and pretty much anyone who would listen for more than five minutes, what was going on and my conspiracy theory. I guess it was almost therapeutic in some way.

Meanwhile, I'm still writing checks everywhere. Money was flying out the door with no end in sight. It was almost three full years later since the inception of this note for a principle balance of $500,000 dollars. The tally to this point was now almost $800,000 dollars. This guy had only made one or two payments the whole time to Walter K. I certainly never received any and it didn't look like any was coming my way anytime soon! This whole fiasco was a joke. I felt there had to be an end to this charade, but when? This guy had the whole court system wrapped up. I felt it in my bones. I knew I was out gunned by a pro and unfortunately, I was learning on the fly. Robert Q. was way ahead of me, playing games and having a good time. Kevin R. never admitted it to me, but I think he felt the same way.

Everyone was demanding money from me. From Kevin R. to our Trustee and their lawyers, the property tax office, credit cards, I mean everyone! Where would it end? I kept my fingers crossed and waited until February

26. That was supposed to be D-Day with the new judge. I was hoping our attorney would get a shot at being the great litigator I hired him for and express our point of view to the court. There was nothing to do but wait and it was sheer torture!

I'd like to share with you a concept I discovered as a tactic to keep the wolves at bay at this point. I call it leapfrogging the calendar. I'd never actually seen it before nor had our attorney either to this magnitude and it kind of goes like this.

I'm sure you've noticed so far that it's fairly easy to schedule a court hearing for 30 days from today. Once a little time goes by, let's say 21 days, you or your attorney does something that requires a continuance, that means additional time and rescheduling with the court. The opposing side won't usually complain either because it's just additional billing hours for him, so rescheduling rarely goes opposed. The court clerk will rarely complain because it doesn't matter to them anyway! If you told your attorney to drag it out, nine times out of ten, it'll be a piece of cake for him or her. The concept is, you keep doing it over and over until you can't get away with it anymore. This is leapfrogging and is a very effective tool at making the bank wait for their money.

For the most part, the court cares more about the poor borrower in distress than the greedy lender. So they will give the borrower as much latitude as possible. The lender, whether private or institutional or otherwise, can simply wait. If the lender doesn't like it? Tough! I realize that now, and there is no changing that mindset. From the clerks to the judges and everyone in between, they are all just working class people like you and me just trying to get by and pay their rent or mortgage and put food on the table, send their kids to school, etc. What they all have in common is that they have to answer to a lender, whether a bank, credit card company, car loans, student loans, mortgages, you name it. So it's natural that the working class population harbor the contempt for the greedy lender they all have to answer to every month.

And truth be told, I kind of feel the same way, so who's to argue? The biggest problem for me and my little organization, is that I'm not swimming in cash all the time. Time tends to work against us in various forms. Allow me to explain.

Sometimes we have a lot of cash, which is a good thing, but it can also be a burden if the cash is sitting idle in some bank account. If our money is doing nothing but generating fees, it's eroding. The trick is to keep rotating the money to make more money to offset the expenses that having money generates. If I or even you for that matter, just left our money in the bank, the bank chisels away at the money just to have it there. At the end of the year, you have to pay the federal government it's share also and anyone else that has their hand in your pocket also.

In this particular case, I'm not an institutional lender, I had much of my own money on the line and I needed to get it back out and don't forget my investor we have to pay back? He was getting very anxious too. How do you think I felt trying to explain all these things going on standing in the way of us getting paid?

I realized, that during this whole time, I sounded like a broken record to my friends and family and especially, my investor, so I got a bright idea. For the next hearing, I would buy one of those little pocket recorders and tape the next court hearing. I figured, this way I could just give everyone I had to report to an audio copy of the hearing and they could hear for themselves what was said and what happened.

On February 25, 2006, we got some good news. In San Diego County, all tentative rulings are published on the internet for anyone interested to see and read the judges opinion on the cases they've heard. Oral arguments are heard a couple of days later after the Judges ruling.

In our case, the judge had denied our borrowers plea for an injunction due to the lack of service on our Trustee. (See, there's that important service process angle again), and of course, Kevin R. and I found it hysterical that Luther L. had dropped the ball. While it was very good news, it was far from victory because

there were still oral arguments to be heard. The outcome can change quickly, and even if you win at this point, the opposing side can still appeal the process and start the whole thing all over again. It's frightening because this option certainly exists. You might not think it's a big deal, but it is when you've got your own money on the line and you're going broke fast!
This is yet another way to make the bank wait for their money.

Also, trust me when I say, that it'll be months before your case is heard again on appeal. So needless to say, I was biting my nails, not exactly jumping up and down for joy just yet, there was still oral arguments to be heard. I called Kevin R. right away and he called Luther L.

Kevin R. wanted to know if they were going to show up for oral arguments and Luther L. said no. I wasn't convinced they were going to throw in the towel that easily. I made sure Kevin R. was aware of my suspicions, and on Friday morning, the day of oral arguments, Kevin R. calls me frantic. You see, Kevin R. usually has Fridays at the office as casual dress day. He told me that he was halfway to his office and he got suspicious. He picked up the phone and called the court clerk to verify that oral arguments for our case had been taken off calendar, which usually means, there's no need to show. The court clerk told him we were still on so Kevin R. called me to tell me he had an hour to go home, put a suit on, and stand in front of the judge. It seemed Luther L. didn't want us to show. This way he would be the only one there and the judge would have to reverse her decision. That sneaky bastard tried to pull a fast one and it almost worked! I quickly got dressed and hightailed it to the courthouse. The service process had stung Luther L. and I was curious to see how he was going to get out of this one.

An hour later, we're standing in front of the judge in court. What does Luther L. do? He tells the judge that he already served everybody including the party in question. I knew it was a lie and I thought for sure we had it in the bag. The judge tell Luther L. that the service process isn't in the file and Luther L. says he has a copy.

The judge wants to see it and Luther L. complies. After some review, she tells him that it's an older service, but she'll accept it. I was floored! Accept it? I couldn't' believe it.

Neither could Kevin R. and he objected right away, but the judge just ignored our attorney. The judge said she would need more time to review this file. We would have to come back in another week to hear the results. Kevin R. again, demanded the bond to secure our position and he cited the civil code that makes the bond mandatory but the judge didn't answer. The judge then dropped the gavel and that was that. It was like some cheesy western where the judge just sentenced some cattle rustler to a hanging. Kevin R. and I walked out of the courtroom dumbfounded, luckily for us, it wasn't over yet. We'd still come back in a week for another shot, but, Robert Q. won again. Oh, remember that 3% interest in our note that we chased around for? Nobody ever said a word or even cared. It was like it didn't ever matter. I smelled a rat and I figured this new judge was also on Luther L.'s list. It was easy to believe because the judge refused to follow the civil procedure code. Maybe she was just trying to cover up for the previous judges mistakes. Either way, our future looked dim.

On the bright side, I was very pleased with the results my trusty recorder provided. It was much easier to explain everything that happened by simply taking the recording of the hearing and giving it to everyone interested. There would be no more, he said-she said. Just the tape of actual events.

So what have we learned here? Plenty I hope? As you can see, delaying the inevitable is actually quite simple. Adding the human factor at the courthouse and capitalizing on the incompetence of the system at work can prove to be fruitful. By making sure everyone follows the rules, checking the service process, paying strict attention to paperwork details and leapfrogging the court calendar, they are extremely effective tools at making the bank wait for their money. As you have seen by my example, I was in a desperate hurry to "move things along" simply because I am a small time operator and have my own money on the line. Most larger institutions you most likely will be dealing with are people who work for a living and are only worried about their jobs. Their own money is not at stake , therefore playing the "delay" game with them will be met with minimal resistance which of course will work wonders in your favor, you just need a little faith.

Chapter 11
Get Me Out!

The following week went by fairly quickly. A couple of days before the hearing, Luther L. had submitted to Kevin R. a settlement offer for $425,000 dollars and of course, I balked. It was pretty much for half of the amount that Robert Q. owed us. It was way too late in the game to just take the money and run. Had he offered that amount in the beginning when I took over, I would've taken it, but at this point, I was already in too deep and gone too far and spent way too much money to just give up. So I turned it down. I was skeptical about the new judge we got to hear our case and Kevin R. tried to convince me that this new judge was on the up and up, I just didn't share his opinion. We were gonna see what that judge had to say in just a couple of days and Kevin R. felt that Robert Q. was now worried and that's why we got a settlement offer and I tried my best to be positive. The morning of the hearing, I put my suit on and made sure my recorder was charged and ready to go.

I had made the mistake of being overly critical about the quality of my previous courtroom audio recording. During playback, it had a lot of static and background noise, so it was difficult to hear the conversations clearly and I felt that I should have been closer to the judge and attorneys so my recorder would capture a cleaner conversation.

I couldn't believe what happen next when our case was to be heard. Kevin R. had just introduced himself to the court when the bailiff noticed my recorder sticking out of my notebook. He walked right over to me and asked me to produce my notebook. He asked me if it was a recording device and I nodded. He then asked me to stand promptly escorted me out the door. He told me that I was now barred from the courtroom.

I always thought the courtroom was a public experience, but guess what? It's not! I figured I'd stay outside and wait for Kevin R. to finish because the suspense was killing me. I snuck into the lobby of the courtroom just outside the doors and I could barely hear what was going on, but what I did hear was the judge instructing the bailiff to confiscate my recorder. Apparently, recorders aren't allowed in the courtroom without permission. So, I quickly made my way to the elevators and out to the parking lot and I thought I was home free when the bailiff ran toward me and caught up with me in the parking lot. He said I'd go to jail if I tried that again and invited me to leave. I said I would, but I didn't go anywhere. I had to wait for Kevin R. because I needed to know the outcome. Half an hour later, Kevin R. walked out into the parking lot with a somber look on his face. First, he had to chastise me for the recorder incident and I acknowledged. The judge wanted to know who I was, but Kevin R. didn't say anything. Apparently, she wanted to hold him accountable for my actions.

After he piped down, he told me the judge didn't rule on the spot. It was Friday, we would have an answer on Monday. Wonderful, I had the whole weekend to sweat it out. When Monday came, I got my answer. The judge clarified not only this hearing but the previous judges decision also and it sort of went like this.

Do you remember when I talked about the first restraining order and how it applied to my previous company? Then I transferred the note in question to the new "Trust" and continued with the foreclosure and Luther L. served the new Trust at David L's office? Well, now the question of valid service was clarified. The new judge amended the previous judge's ruling to include all successors or assigns, meaning, the judge wrapped my first company and the new trust together as one so now the restraining order applied to the new "Trust" also. That part seemed to be written to appease Robert Q. and his attorney. The second part of the judge's ruling did in fact provide for a bond to protect our position. The bond was set for $25,000 dollars, which was a total slap in the face to us. Normally a bond is set to cover the indebtedness and at this point was somewhere around $800,000. It wasn't even enough to cover half of the legal fees alone and I was crushed and felt officially beaten. Kevin R. couldn't believe it either and I figured it was because of the recorder incident. Kevin R. said it was highly unlikely but I didn't believe him. Kevin R. said we still had another shot. He had taken the initiative and already scheduled another hearing for April 21, 2006. He said we should get what we're looking for by then. A couple of days later, just to add insult to injury, the first lien holder sends me a notice to tell me that Robert Q. hasn't made any payments in two months totaling about $25,000 dollars and frankly, I couldn't take much more. I was so sick of it all. I went home and drank myself into a coma. I was so disappointed and disillusioned. What was I dealing with here? More corruption? It was easy to believe and it sure seemed like it. Kevin R. told me that in the thirty years of practicing law, he had never seen anything like what was happening in this case. He was now convinced beyond the shadow of a doubt that the peculiarities in these courtrooms were suspect. Was it corruption we were dealing with? Or just the high and mighty syndrome you get from being a judge? Corruption? But how do you prove it?

On Kevin R's part, several other cases in front of the same judges he had were going the same way. Judges were ruling totally one-sided, not hearing certain facts or even oral arguments, so he quickly moved all his cases that were scheduled in these same courtrooms to other courtrooms. Our attorney, Kevin R. was finally catching on.

The Trustee I hired to do this foreclosure was very quick to submit more invoices to me that their attorney wanted paid. They hadn't even done anything to help, yet they wanted money from me. In fact, this whole fiasco was caused by the Trustee I hired. I trusted them to not make any mistakes, yet here we were knee deep in it! I didn't want any part of these obstacles, that's why I hired them in the first place and they screwed me too. I didn't know what to do. So a couple of days later, I was going through court records and I found a new lawsuit against Robert Q. Big surprise! This time, it was a law firm that was suing Robert Q.? So, I pulled the file to see what it was all about and as it turns out, this law firm had represented Robert Q. while he had a very popular restaurant in San Diego at the marina. He was being evicted for nonpayment of rent totaling two years. This law firm represented our borrower and had successfully made a deal with the landlord to keep the restaurant going.

I paid the law firm a visit and after introductions, they gave me the whole story. They said that Robert Q. was having difficulties with his business and paying the rent on the restaurant at the marina in San Diego and the Port Authority wanted to shut him down. Instead, the attorneys were trying to help our poor borrower by patching things up and working it out with the Port Authority, and months later, just when everything seemed to be ironed out, Robert Q. pulled the plug and just disappeared, owing the lawyers just over $90,000 dollars in legal fees. What I wanted to know was why the tab got so large? Why didn't they just quit? I was curious. Every other lawyer I've ever encountered wanted to quit as soon as we got close to within $1,000.00 of expended legal fees, but $90,000.00? Jesus! That's a lot of unpaid legal fees!

Well, as it turns out, they couldn't quit. Apparently, the lawyer's have to get a judges approval to do so and nonpayment of legal fees isn't grounds enough to get a release from the case. I thought that was interesting and it seems like an easy way to get a lawyer to work for free? Just give him a little retainer, and don't pay him on the rest. Interesting. Anyway, another interesting fact these lawyers told me while exchanging information on our borrower was, the court system. Unfortunately, our venue already has fame. They simply stated that they don't do business in that district. They told me that particular court system does peculiar things and it's not a level playing field. My suspicions had been confirmed and I thanked them and quickly excused myself. I felt it was time to think of a quick and painless exit strategy.

April 21, 2006 was coming up quick and the deadline for the service process on everyone involved was a few days away. I went to Kevin R.'s office to make sure everyone, and I mean everyone, had been served. I was assured time and again everything was fine, not to worry, so on and so on. I looked at the file at Kevin R.'s office and noticed something odd. It seemed that Robert Q. had now filed pro se. Pro se in legal terms means, he's representing himself, but Robert Jr. is still with Luther L. I asked Kevin R. about it and he said it was all taken care of. On D-Day morning, April 21, 2006, our case was to be heard again and this time, with an impending victory, and of course as suspected, we get the bomb. The tentative ruling had been posted on the court calendar website. Our case had been disqualified because of lack of service upon, get this, of all people, Robert Q., because he was filing "pro se" or rather, representing himself, was not served and of course, I was horrified to say the least, and then naturally infuriated! This was precisely what I was trying to avoid! I immediately called Kevin R. to find out what happened and it seems that his secretary overlooked the service process on our borrower. I was even more disappointed to find him smug about the whole mistake. Even after me hounding him about the service process, pointing out Robert Q.'s filing in pro se, they forget to serve the guy we were after, Robert Q., of all people! I couldn't believe it!

Not only was I staring at defeat, and a probable bankruptcy, but now dissension among the ranks? Kevin R. decided he was now bailing out on me. He said to me to just sue him for the mistake and hung up on me. That was that. Robert Q. knew that by representing himself, there would be no way to serve him and after I got over the thoughts of a quick and painless suicide, I secretly praised Robert Q. for the move. It was brilliant!

After an entire year of going back and forth with legal mumbo-jumbo and tens of thousands of dollars worth of legal fees, I was no closer to getting paid today than I was almost a year ago. The funny thing is, when I talked to our Trustee about this whole thing a couple of days later, they said the filings for restraining orders and preliminary injunctions had skyrocketed at the county court level. It seems that our little case pretty much set the precedent for all future cases of this type to come. Early May, I got another offer from Luther L. to settle, but this time it was a little different. It seemed that the first lien holder was interested in refinancing us out of this fiasco, so I called them.

The main man, Glen F., definitely wanted to talk to me. It seemed that Robert Q. had been trying to convince him to buy us out and Glen F. told me Robert

Q. was definitely rattled, between all the court dates and files about him I was passing around, he wanted me to go away. Frankly, I agreed with him in respect to wanting out also. I'd had enough. The ass-kicking we'd taken through this whole endeavor had me completely worn out. When I first spoke to Glen F., I thought for sure he was going to try to squeeze me for some cash. I was already thinking this guy might want me to make the $12,000 a month mortgage payments to protect my position and I was already prepared to do so when the exact opposite happened. After a lengthy conversation, it sort of went like this: he was well aware of all the trouble I was having with our borrower, and wasn't in a big hurry to get involved. He offered me a few outs. The first out was, I could continue making the mortgage payments of $12,000 as long as necessary without worry about acceleration, meaning him calling the note due for whatever reason.

With the second option, he would refinance the entire balance of the first mortgage of 1.4 million dollars and my now $800,000 dollars, after I was able to foreclose on our borrower and take possession of the property. The only problem I had with that was that I didn't see that option materializing any time soon. Even if we did foreclose, Robert Q. would come back with a wrongful foreclosure lawsuit just to piss me off and to squeeze another six months to a year of free house out of me. I knew that at the very least, he would fight me on the eviction. Just fighting the eviction alone would buy him at least another six months. The third and final option was for Glen F. to buy me out. I liked that one best. I wanted out anyway! He was offering a fair price. Not a great price, but fair enough and I waited a few days to say anything. I took him up on the offer. It was time to pull the plug. Considering I'd only paid a fraction of the face value for the note and I'd spent approximately $70,000 in legal fees by this point along with other expenses related, that meant that we would gross enough money to pretty much walk away even and maybe a little extra. It wasn't a bad payday, certainly more than working a normal job, but not the million we were looking for, but by this point, it was good enough.

This meant we weren't losing and frankly, I couldn't take any more abuse.

My investor, was extremely anxious to say the least. I didn't tell him about our buy-out offer, not to conceal it from him, but because I didn't think it would actually go through and I didn't want to get his hopes up. I set the closing date for the beginning of May 2006. We went back and forth with the agreements and paperwork for a couple of weeks and some very long sleepless nights. I was crossing my fingers and toes hoping this wouldn't fall apart at the end. I was extremely helpful and very accommodating to say the least. Why? Because there wouldn't be anyone else out there that would buy this note from me for that kind of money with all this litigation going on. I had to be very accommodating whether I liked it or not!

Glen F. set me up with his escrow agent and it seemed he had used them many times before for other transactions. Apparently, he had faith in their ability as an escrow office to handle this transaction. His escrow officer was very helpful and knowledgeable about very little of our transaction. She didn't know the first thing on how to handle ours. But of course, I helped her. What was I going to do, walk out? And just on a personal note, I have come to find that when you are buying or selling a mortgage or deed of trust, whatever your state calls them, don't be surprised to find how little the escrow people know about your transaction. So don't rely on them for help. They are only there to facilitate. You are definitely on your own on these, so watch yourself. You could get taken very easily!

On the day of closing, I was going to do it alone. My wife was wringing her fists with anticipation and I couldn't blame her, so I took her with me and I'm glad I did. The escrow office barely had half of the paperwork ready and I had to reprint everything. And because I had to reprint everything, my wife would have to resign all the documents. I sure was happy I brought her along! The escrow officer was very apologetic and very sweet and she assured me the transaction would go through. I thought she had a check for me but as it turned out, for that kind of money, they only did wire transfers. It figures, it was Friday on a three day weekend, of course, which meant that we had to wait until the following Tuesday afternoon to find out if we got burned. Wonderful! Jeez.. let's party anyway...

I called Glen F. and he assured me the money was there. The escrow officer assured me the money was there but I wasn't so optimistic, although, I had to give them the benefit of the doubt. Do you blame me? I'd been raked over the coals so many times, it was kind of hard to remain positive about the whole transaction. Who could blame me?

My wife and I sort of celebrated our impending victory. Tuesday morning came around and after biting our nails and checking our bank account online, sure enough the money was there, and we were officially out! So, like all good little boys and girls do, we drank ourselves into a coma that evening and slept ever so soundly. We had made it though, we got paid and still turned a profit!

So what did we learn from this chapter? Do you understand what I mean about dragging out the process to a point where the lender just throws in the towel and wants out? You can accomplish the same with patience. Once a loan is sold to some other unsuspecting investor, the process starts all over again, only now, you are better informed and already know what's coming around the corner. Most lenders will give loans away that have litigation and disputes involved. You can capitalize in a multitude of ways. One of them being is that you can buy your own loan for pennies on the dollar. Another would be to negotiate a short payoff for pennies on the dollar with the current lender. If your loan is sold to someone else during the litigation, dispute the whole thing!

Chapter 12
More Loose Ends

Why is it, that when we think the nightmare is finally over, it's not? Sometimes, life's little lessons just want to keep on teaching! Well, I certainly had a difficult time in putting this whole thing to rest or rather, out of my life. I'll show you what I mean.

I went to see Kevin R., our attorney, to settle up with him and was very happy for me and he was glad we were out. However, the lawsuit was still pending. Luther L. had sent a settlement agreement to me to sign and in it was excusing everyone from the lawsuit except me. It said I should pay for everybody's attorney fees. I balked. I certainly wasn't going to agree to that trash so I took the agreement and a fat tip marker and scratched that part out and sent it back. Of course, we went back and forth for a good three months before the case was finally dismissed. But I didn't pay too much attention. I was out and no longer responsible.

I thought I had already settled with our Trustee also, but the problem was, their attorney kept generating more fees to review the settlement agreement to get them out, so it was up to me to just pay. It was a constant fee this and fee that. I said no! As predicted, they threatened to sue me and I dared them. I had washed my hands of everyone involved that wanted money from me from this case, but they refused to let it go. The last time I spoke with Kevin R., he had told the attorney for our Trustee to just let it go. After all, it was because of their negligence that we got into this whole mess to begin with. He told them not to provoke me any longer or I would surely win a lawsuit against them in the future with unspecified damages. I never heard another word from anyone related to this case again nor did I want to hear from anyone anyway and I certainly didn't care. My investor was understandably hot and heavy for me to give him his money back. He actually took the offensive and blamed me for everything that had happened. He was very upset with me about this whole thing, as if I had planned it somehow, so I obliged and gave him his money and profit he was entitled to.

As of the initial writing in February 2007, I was contemplating the closure of this writing and wondered what ever happened with our former borrower, Robert

Q.? I was looking at county records over the internet the other day and I typed Robert Q.'s name into the computer and as it turned out, a Notice of Default was filed by Glenn F., the people who purchased the note from me on our borrower Mr. Robert Q. Apparently, our borrower must've stopped making payments back in September or October of 2006 to the new lender, just after the lawsuit was dismissed. It looks like he's doing it all over again, only with Glenn F. this time. Once in foreclosure, always in foreclosure and don't you forget it!

As I was driving down the freeway the other day, I was scrolling through my address book in my cell phone and ran across Robert Q's old phone number and I dialed it just out of curiosity. I figured I'd give him a call to thank him for the lessons he taught me about a "different" kind of world. Lo' and behold, he actually answered his phone. I identified myself and promptly thanked him, he responded by saying he didn't understand the nature of the phone call so I elaborated a little.

The funny thing about this conversation was the turn of events. Robert Q. told me that I set things in motion that would be difficult for him to recover from but first, he told me he had a stoke and was slowly recovering. With therapy, his speech was gradually returning to almost normal. The second subject were the restaurants. I had sent in the complaints to the Alcoholic Beverage Control office about them granting a liquor license to a suspended corporation and as turns out, they actually revoked his liquor licenses and he had to close two restaurants. He was currently in litigation over a couple of other restaurants with the sellers because of the information I had sent them about his career, and he didn't appreciate the interview with the FBI either. He wanted to know why I would do such things? Why I asked? I told him I just wanted to be paid so I could go on my way and about my business.

What I was dying to know from him and couldn't think of a better way to ask, was where he learned to manipulate the legal system and everything else? What he told me next changed the way I look at many of my business ventures today. He said to me that it was just a method of survival and the minimum level of survival you are willing to accept. He certainly had a valid point and some thought, I understood completely. Another statement or rather admission he made to me that made my day, and to this day still rings in my ears, was that he said that he completely underestimated me. Had he known earlier I would go through such lengths to get his attention, he would have just paid me off sooner.

    I didn't say anything about the default with Glenn F. but I guess I didn't have to. I had tried to warn him from day one to just pay me. So I guess what he got in the end, some people would call poetic justice.
By now, you should have a thorough understanding by way of example how a seemingly innocuous homeowner literally "made the bank wait for their money and there was nothing the bank could do but wait."

    In this last chapter of the story of what actually happened to me, is a shining example of the banker throwing in the towel which is all too common these days. This chapter is chocked full of examples to learn by and I charge you to go back and reread it when you can. Should the need arise, remember that the name of the game is delay-delay-delay. Mortgages and loans are bought and sold everyday of the year and many are sold for pennies on the dollar. In the following and last chapter of this book, I will explain in easy to understand details the mechanics of the system of the sale and transfer of mortgages from originator to seller to buyer and so forth. You will understand the required notices anytime a change in title takes place. Also, should the need present itself, included will be strategies and remedies that are available to you through the legal system that were in place long before I ever stepped into the business world.

CHAPTER 13
HAVE YOU SEEN MY NOTE?

As of this writing, January 2011, the sub-prime mortgage disaster of 2008 is all but a distant memory. There have been millions of foreclosures taken place across the country with no end in sight in just about every corner and every neighborhood in America. The foreclosures have not isolated themselves to just the sub-prime borrowers but "A" credit borrowers as well. Hundreds of thousands of families have been displaced and or left homeless and many more will suffer the wrath as well. The lenders responsible for so many of the foreclosures are sitting smug with their coffers filled to the brim with taxpayer cash. We are enjoying a Presidential and Congressional administration that could care less about Main St. America as is evident not by the rhetoric, but by shining examples and actions.

The horrible part of this housing melt-down currently underway across the country is that it all could have been minimized and kept under tight control. I was interviewed by a Bloomberg Television reporter in March of 2008 and was asked point blank if the mortgage mess could be corrected and I admitted that indeed there were remedies. Unfortunately, my answers fell upon deaf ears. As I have witnessed the disintegration of my country and clearly am also witnessing the widening divide between the haves and have-nots. I've felt compelled to rewrite this little book and add some powerful and very useful information to it's contents to show my readers that there are indeed remedies to stalling and challenging a foreclosure action. But what if that foreclosure action has already taken place? Well there are remedies for that too and I am prepared to show you where they are.

I must admit that I have for many years, harbored nothing but contempt toward the banks and their staff, the U.S. Post Office and let's not forget the Department of Motor Vehicles. There is nothing I can do about the U.S. Post Office other than wait for the media to announce the Federal bailout in their favor any time soon. Personally, I think they should have sold to Federal Express in the late eighties when they had the chance and they had a willing buyer. As you might have guessed, I worked for the Post Office for a short while after serving in the the United States Navy and in the infamous words of Donald Trump, "the people of the Post Office are great... at doing something else." And I have to agree.

As far as the DMV is concerned, they are so poorly run it's fascinating to watch the staggering levels of incompetence. I'm not just talking about the DMV in California, it's a nationwide epidemic. But the banks, well here we actually have a chance to make a difference and I'm pleased to share with you the system. You may or may not be skeptical and if you are, you should be! If you're not, then shame on you! You probably believe everything the mainstream media have to say and the tooth fairy.

I would like to begin by explaining to you in detail how loans/mortgages/Deeds of Trust, how the sale and transfer of these loans take place between seller and buyer. For the purpose of this discussion, I will generalize so as to present to you a "big picture" so to speak. Please follow along with me and should you need to stop and reread, by all means do so. The information I am about to share with you could prove to be quite valuable to you in the near future, so a thorough understanding is imperative, but not to worry, it isn't rocket-science.

When a borrower applies to a lender/mortgage broker for a loan/mortgage to buy a house to live in, he identifies a property and he fills out and submits a loan application to see how much he qualifies for and the would-be lender goes to work and tries to find an investor that will fund this loan. Investors come in all sizes and shapes and sometimes these investors are pension funds, mutual funds, larger banks, insurance companies and the list goes on and on. When the broker goes through his list and finds a suitable investor willing to fund the loan, he goes back to the borrower to give the good news. The buyer agrees and they move forward with the purchase of the new house. When the buyer/borrower sits down at escrow to sign documents, very rarely does he know what exactly he's signing. All he usually cares about is his new house and the monthly payments. In the settlement statement, there are fees added for the processing of the "loan" in question.

Those fees go to different people in the circle of the real estate business such as an appraiser, realtor, escrow office, document prep, the mortgage broker and everyone else which are paid by the borrower. But where does the money for the loan come from? It comes from the investor that has committed to buy the loan being funded. Generally these days, if you look closely at the loan documents, they will be written in favor of the loan broker which will then commit to "sell" the loan to the investor. So, the borrower signs on the dotted line and gets the keys to the house and copies of everything and celebrates. The broker celebrates too because he just got paid his "discount fees" which are anything but discounted and the investor picked up a new loan.

But what happens to the loan after that? Well, the borrower gets a statement every month from a loan servicer which takes his payments and distributes them to the appropriate channels. The investor might keep this loan in their portfolio for an undetermined period of time or they just might package that loan with several others, sometimes even in the thousands and sell them as securities on the stock market.

But what are securities? The illustration below shows that a set of securities are like a freshly baked pie. In that pie are slices of numerous sizes and shapes. When an investor is interested in this type of security, he will choose a slice of the pie that fits his appetite. Sometimes that appetite is small or can be quite large. Those investors will buy into these securities with real money and receive payments based on a predetermined rate of return, every month or every year. This is why your loan most likely have changed hands over the years. It has gone from one owner to another for an infinite number of reasons.

Let's stop right here and look at the transaction of transfer itself and it is also illustrated for you below.

The new loan was written in favor of the loan broker(1), then was sold and bought by the first investor (2).

Investor number one, sold your loan along with several others to other investors (3) on Wall Street as securities or maybe to another investor. So that's three transactions or changes in ownership and title of your loan.

Now let's take a look at how title of loans from one investor to another are conveyed.

In the sale of loans by investors in the secondary market, there are required pieces of documentation that accompany every loan transfer and the omission or incomplete documentation are grounds for an unsuccessful transaction between parties and they are as follows:

1. Purchase and Sale agreement
2. Original Promissory Note
3. Original Deed of Trust or Mortgage
4. Allonge (which conveys the legal right for the purchaser to receive payments)
5. Assignment of Deed of Trust or Mortgage (filed at the county recorders office in the county where the property is located and the original is returned to the new owner of the loan. This shows the world that the loan in question has a new owner)
6. Estoppel letter (statement certifying correct amounts due and payable by the borrower)
7. Loan accounting of payments received and due or payable
8. Amortization schedule
9. Lenders Title Policy
10. Lenders Insurance Policy
11. Property tax accounting
12. All borrowers pertinent information.

First, an agreement or contract is typed up and signed by both parties where price and method of delivery are foremost.

Second, all original documentation is reviewed for accuracy and validity usually verified.

Third, an assignment of mortgage, Note Allonge and Estoppel Letters are written in favor of the new investor.

Funds are then exchanged and all of the above documentation is also exchanged and the homeowner gets a letter in the mail to let him know where to send all future payments. See? Quite simple. Normally, the only real evidence that a loan sale has taken place is at the county level where the assignment is "supposed to" be recorded. Notice I said "supposed to?" Assuming this property was purchased by our borrower in San Diego County California and let's say this loan is for sale and I'm doing my due-diligence before committing to buy and verifying that all information is true and correct. Normally, I could go to property records at the county offices and verify the chain of title of the loan in question.   I need to make sure that this loan is actually owned by the seller and no shenanigans are taking place, so I look for the originating broker's "assignment" to investor number one and check my copy of the document against the recorded document. If found correct, I then proceed and look for the "assignment" of the loan from investor number one to investor number two, the current note holder and seller. If found correct and all other document is in acceptable order and condition, I go ahead and make the purchase. Investor number two would take the new assignment in my favor and record the document and eventually the county clerk will mail the original back to me in a couple of weeks and the homeowner would get a letter in the mail notifying him of where to send all future payments. This concludes an over simplified explanation of a loan sale. Was it complicated? No, of course not, so long as you know what to look for and expect.

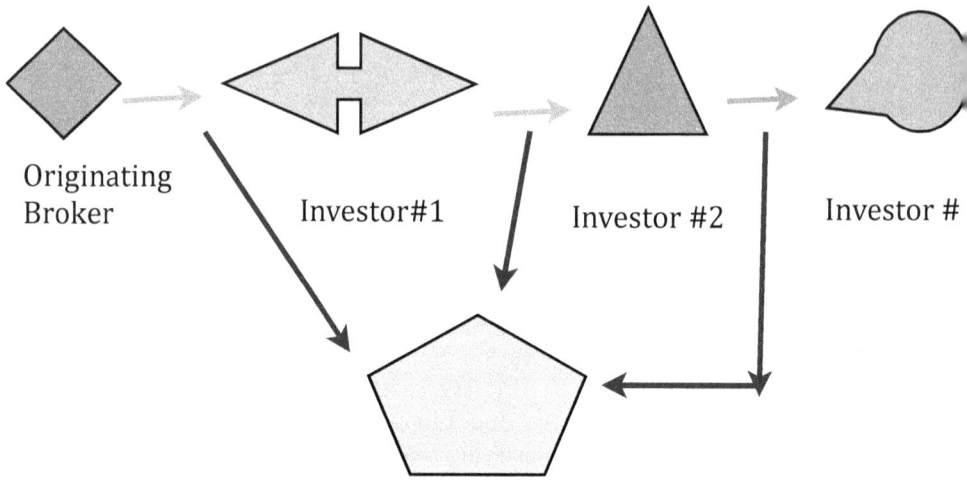

County Recorder/
Clerks Office

Grey Arrows = Assignments to be recorded

Black Arrows = Sale and Transfers

As you can see, it's not a complicated process, just a time-consuming and cumbersome one. This is how notes have been traded since the early part of the last century and of course, just about every state in the union has legislation that governs how these transactions are to take place. There are also rules in place that govern what you can and can't do, and we'll get to that in just a moment.

Now for a little history and back-tracking. After the last stock market bubble had popped in the late 1990's and many investors lost vast fortunes by the "pie in the sky" promises start-up internet companies offered, that unsuspecting investors (suckers) were reeled into the ingenious investment bankers web on Wall Street's newest rally. The latest and greatest investment vehicle that could be easily sold to investors worldwide in order to generate gargantuan fees and was totally secure. But investors worldwide were rightfully skittish and weren't about to open their checkbooks right away for just any product. President Bush at the time went on a campaign to house America. He wanted every American to own a home and in my opinion, I agree and still agree that every American and his family should own their own home. It might not be the Taj Mahal, but a roof over yours and your families heads to call home is imperative for the safety and sanity of our country.

The Wall Street geniuses focused their attention and decided to capitalize on this campaign and came up with ingenious ways to sell what they referred to as, Mortgage-Backed Securities(MBS's) to investors worldwide. These securities imply to investors that their investment in products like these are safe and sound, not risky like those tech stocks, but safe because they are all backed by real estate in the United States of America.

And because we have certain "underwriting standards" to be met, only the most creditworthy would qualify for a mortgage to buy a house. Therefore, safety was paramount. In the beginning of the big push for mortgages, investors worldwide liked the idea of safety versus the volatility and the lure of easy money of the stock market, so these products became ver popular and generated handsome fees for the sellers of the mortgage-backed securities. Of course, the demand for these products coupled with low interest rates, sky-rocketed and soon there weren't enough mortgage backed securities's to be had. Wall Street, mind you, wants everything to work at lightning speed, so there was still a huge underlying problem in the antiquated system of due-diligence and the proper filing of the paperwork transferring loans/notes from seller to buyer. In order to generate those fees as fast as possible, keep in mind we're referring to hundreds of millions of dollars every year, the due-diligence and filing of documents and the bottle-neck at the respective county recorders or government offices in Anytown, USA, had to be altered or removed. So how was it done?

First, as far as due-diligence of the mortgage pools was concerned, waiting for prospective buyers of your(if your the seller) pool of loans to be looked at and mulled over by a fickle buyer or buyers is obviously not only extremely time consuming, but just down right irritating. So the solution was to give copies of these pools of loans to an independent third party that would audit and give each pool a grade ranging from AAA all the way down the scale to the equivalent of toilet-paper. Obviously, the higher the credit rating of the pool, the higher the security and safety and less likely-hood of default, the higher the price tag or fees generated. This system of credit rating worked well in the beginning stages until the volume of AAA borrowers began to diminish and so did those fees, so something had to be done.

Second, enter Mortgage Electronic Registration Systems or MERS for short. Founded in 1995, was the banking industries' answer to the cumbersome and time-consuming process of transferring loans from seller to buyer and so on and so forth. They would serve as a registry for loans to be held in escrow or "trust" for the lack of a better description. The beneficial interests (owner) of those loans would change from time to time but the Trustee or in some cases as MERS refers to itself, "Nominee" would stay the same.

Supposedly, each loan that was registered in the MERS system got an ID number assigned to it and this number would follow the life of the loan through payoff or foreclosure no matter how many times that loan changed hands over the years.

Another added "benefit" of utilizing the MERS system was the elimination or rather, circumventing of filing fees that are generated each and every time an assignment of mortgage or deed of trust is filed. Only now as of this writing are the cash strapped municipalities across the nation starting to realize they have been duped out of millions of dollars in required filing fees by the banking industry and I believe it's only a matter of time before these cities begin attacking and demanding from MERS and the lenders for reimbursement of those fees. But, that another subject.

When I first encountered the MERS system in the early part of the year 2000, I didn't really understand their role in the mortgage industry or why they even existed. I couldn't even find anyone that could explain to me what the role MERS was playing, but what I did know about it was that their system is fundamentally flawed, yet just about every lender that has sold mortgage pools to an investor/buyer has utilized the MERS system so I ignored it and went about my business. I guess I was the odd man out?
The illustration below might help clarify the role that "MERS" as a "Trust" supposedly plays.

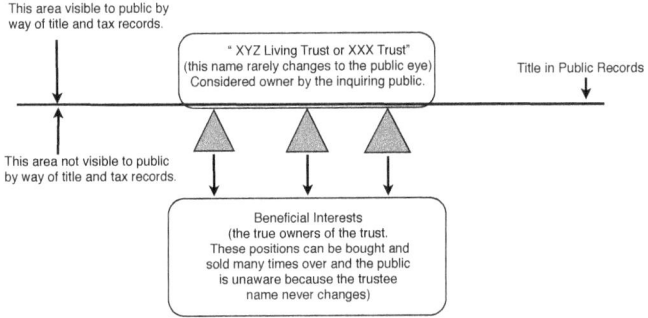

Enter sub-prime lending. I'm sure that at this point, you are pretty familiar with what that term means by now. In case you don't, it simply means, "borrowers with a less than stellar credit rating that still get loans." That's it. Sub-prime was any type of higher interest than normal lending that a buyer would agree to. Sub-prime lending used to pay the mortgage brokers quite well in discount points and fees, as long as the buyer got into the house they thought they could never have, the buyer would go for it and sign just about anything!

Because of an appreciating market in many cities across our country, loan fees and discount points and especially down-payments were all rolled into the loan and the price of the house. Then the borrower could get himself a house simply by signing on the dotted line. It didn't really matter if the borrower could actually afford to make those house payments for an extended period of time. His loan was going to be packaged and sold off as securities very soon after closing anyway so it really didn't matter. The loan broker mentality was, "let somebody else worry about it!"

But, even those borrowers started to become scarce and Wall Street and the banks needed to make more loans. Keep in mind, Wall Street is all about generating fees. So they came up with wonderful loan products to fit just about any size of loan and budget. The most popular and toxic were the interest-only type where the borrower only pays the interest on his loan and doesn't touch the principle.

And of course the infamous negative amortization loans where the borrower has choices every month on whether to make a regular principle and interest payment on his loan, or to just pay a fraction of the interest payment due where the remainder of the amortized payment was tacked on to the principle of his loan. So every month, the borrowers loan would increase in principle due, not by much, but it did increase, hence the name, negative amortization. These loans also carried with them a teaser rate where the initial two or three years would have a very low and unrealistic interest rate and payments, but then would reset higher after a predetermined period of time had passed.   As for the borrower, not to worry, when the loan was to reset higher and payments were scheduled to increase, he could always refinance later. And if the property increased in value by appreciation, well he could borrow against the house to pay off some bills or go on vacation or maybe buy a new car. It didn't matter, because these loans where going to be sold off on Wall Street anyway to some unsuspecting and faceless investor. These loans were _never_ meant to be repaid down to zero, they were only a ticket to ride for right now.

If the borrower got himself into serious trouble, he could always sell the house to the next sucker that was willing to pay top dollar, and because the house had appreciated in value, he could take his new equity and buy a new house and start the process all over again.

Now let's change gears and talk a little about the realities of the recording process of loan documents at the county recorders office in Anytown, USA.

When a borrower refinances with a new loan or becomes a new homeowner, he signs on the dotted line and off he goes to carry his bride over the threshold, what happens to the documentation after that? Well, there are certain critical elements of the paperwork that require specific attention. First would be the Deed from the previous owner to the new owner conveying title from previous owner to the new owner, and second would be the Deed of Trust or Mortgage the homeowner has just signed and are both sent to the county recorder for recording to become part of the official record for that county. Those documents, once recorded, eventually get sent back to either the escrow office or the originating lender and in this case, the mortgage broker several weeks later.

The other documents like the Promissory Note and other disclosures are given to the investor which funded the new loan. A few weeks later when the investor sells his pool of "notes" to another investor as securities, the paperwork is sent and forwarded along and is filed away somewhere presumably safe. Then, as this is slowly happening and weeks later, the documents from the county recorder show up in the mail to the originating broker. He is then supposed to forward them on to the investor who bought the loan to accompany the loan documents supposedly in their possession. But the investor has already forwarded all those loan documents on, so the processor who received the documents at investor #1's office, lets them sit on his desk for awhile before sending them on to catch up with the file of original documentation. By the time that processor has done his job, the original file of loan documents have now become even harder to find.

Should you ever decide to engage in the business of buying and selling mortgages, you will inevitably become accustomed to how incomplete the files are for the loans you are buying. The list of documentation for the loans originated as I outlined for you in earlier chapters? You'd be lucky to find half that information in the file. Many of these critical documents never find their corresponding file, ever.

Now that we have a very basic understanding of the mortgage buy/sell process, let's look at how it relates to our task at hand at "making the bank wait."

When a borrower stops making his mortgage payments for an infinite number of reasons, the loan servicer puts the borrower on notice and theoretically tries to help/accommodate the customer. Internally at the loan servicer's location, wherever that may be, the borrower's file is put into a delinquent status and as time goes on, then moves into what we call default stage and presumably, now "Loss-Mitigation" gets involved to deal with the borrower in order to mitigate losses, hence "loss-mitigation." As you might have guessed, a loan in default requires much more attention now that different departments and organizations must now get involved. This under/non-performing loan now has much more attention than it truly deserves and of course, begins to drain the loan owner of any kind of future positive returns. This is now the foreclosure process.

Eventually, if the homeowner/borrower does nothing to cure the default and impending foreclosure, the property will be sold at auction. Depending on the local real estate market conditions, most likely a sale for a fraction of the unpaid balance will take place.

In some states, the law allows the foreclosing lender to attempt to collect the deficiency which is the difference of the price the property was able to bring at auction and the remainder of the unpaid balance plus all legal costs associated with the foreclosure action. In some cases, these deficiencies can run into the tens and even hundreds of thousands of dollars. The lender sues the previous homeowner for the difference and if the homeowner/ borrower does nothing, the lender will win by default, a judgment against the borrower for that amount plus attorneys fees and other costs associated with the action. How's that for adding insult to injury? Now the homeowner/borrower has become a debtor and this judgment will chase him around for the next few years, usually about 10. But not to worry, we'll show you how to deal with that judgment in just a minute. So, what can you do about this whole mess?

Well as it turns out, there are very simple ways of delaying the inevitable, And if delayed long enough, the lender will stop trying to collect from the homeowner/borrower/debtor because it costs money to try and collect. As ridiculous as it may sound, all the debtor has to really do is avoid the service process. To do so, the debtor should probably change his contact information long before it is actually necessary. Perhaps as the borrower sees an impending situation that will most likely require the use of these tactics.
Other more aggressive stall tactics can be used such as the ones you've already read about in previous chapters, but the most aggressive and manipulative, lies with <u>*demanding from the lender, complete and original documentation of the loan documents you signed in escrow and above all, proof of chain of title with original recorded mortgage assignments and Allonges*</u>. You must demand chain of title because some sympathetic courts have begun to allow foreclosing lenders to continue with a foreclosure action despite lack of proper evidence and faulty record keeping. So demanding chain of title is that which proves to the world who owns that loan and it is a feat that is unattainable anywhere. If your loan has changed hands at least twice in it's history since inception and MERS was involved in the loan documents and should you decide to stay and fight the foreclosure, eventually you will win! But you will require the services of competent legal counsel to achieve success. Never forget and always keep in mind that in the legal system, details are imperative! You will have no choice but to play by the rules set forth, so in my opinion, what's good for the goose, is good for the gander! They(the foreclosing lenders) must also have to play by the rules and don't forget, so do the Judges. Proper documentation is critical and I cannot stress it enough! Should you encounter a Judge(s) that is ignoring the law and procedures of law, it is not only your duty, but civic duty to file the appropriate

complaints with the state judicial review board. It won't be pretty, but I'm telling you, it is your duty! If that Judge feels he or she is above the law, make them answer to it! If you don't believe me, just look into it, there are always judges being disbarred and carted off to jail for an infinite number of reasons. The question to ask is, how long did they get away with ignoring the law until finally someone complained?

But what if you've already been foreclosed upon and your house is long gone? You've moved away somewhere new and hopefully better. It just so happens that you've read this book and are wondering if it's too late to do anything about it? Is it too late? My answer is no! Definitely not and not by a long-shot! Please allow me to explain.

In the great state of California, despite the record number of foreclosures that have taken place, many of those should not have been completed. Why? Well, chain of title! It's that simple yet so complex that this very concept will dangerously and literally bring the financial house down! Ninety percent of the foreclosures that have taken place where the loan in question has changed hands and yet no evidence of any transactions taking place, have been filed at the county level never actually had the authority to foreclose their loans. How do I know this?

Because every loan I ever purchased from a lending institution came without a chain of title. Any time I went to restructure some homeowners loan that was bought for pennies on the dollar? There was never any question as to whom I was and under what authority I undertaking. No one ever questioned my ownership of their loan, no one ever questioned my authority to restructure their loan and no one ever questioned my authority to reinstate or reconvey their loan. No homeowner, no title company, no attorneys, no Judges, no one! They just assumed... and that is exactly what is happening in America today because no one knows the real truth behind the process!

So what can you do if you've been foreclosed upon? Well, that's an excellent question that requires a very detailed answer. Let's start with identifying the state laws we will be working with. In the great state of California, whether you agree with me or not, when it comes to the subject of quiet title litigation, the rest of the 49 states in our glorious union are all pretty much the same except for some minor differences here and there. I charge you with finding out for yourself what kind of latitude you will have. I will explain to you the process by example of a "quiet title action."

    Let's say, your home was foreclosed upon a year ago by the third or fourth lender you made your payments to during your time of ownership. You moved out and moved on with your life. You know that your old house was sold at auction to some investor at the courthouse steps. That investor purchased your old house, then painted and carpeted and maybe replaced some appliances. He then listed the house with a realtor and the house eventually sold for a profit for the investor and now the new homeowners are happy in their new home. There are now two transactions that have taken place between you, the old lender, and the current homeowner. But what does this have to do with you? That's a great question and it all starts with, it depends. It depends on what you are after. What if I told you or you found out later that the lender that foreclosed on your home never even had the authority to do so? What if I told you that the lender, didn't even own your loan? What if I told you that lender didn't even exist? What would you do then? What remedies would you have? In short, Quiet title.

    In the State of California, there is a statute of limitations of five years. This means you have up to five years to lay claim, to bring a quiet title action against the current homeowner. No, it doesn't mean you'll get your old house back, but what it does mean is that you just might be compensated for a wrongful foreclosure action from the previous lender! Now isn't that something worth thinking about?

    In short, the way it works is that first you need to know if the foreclosing lender even had the authority to foreclose on you? If not, then you bring a quiet title action against the new homeowner. You <u>will</u> require the services of competent legal counsel for this action. As soon as the current homeowner gets "served"(there's that service process again), he runs to his attorney which directs him to the title company that issued a title policy when they purchased the house from the investor. After some hemming and hawing, the title company will want to settle with you so you'll go away and you will, for an undetermined amount of money. That title company will look to the previous title policy for reimbursement and then that previous title company will look to the foreclosing lender for reimbursement and you better believe, they'll get it! Why will they get it and why should they compensate you? All to avoid trial, that's why. Do you know how hard it would be for a lender to find and unbiased jury these days? Think about it?

The good thing is, you will now have money in your pocket to straighten out your finances and move on with your life! And of course, make some better choices for you and your family. How does that sound?

The section of the law in California is called <u>Judicial Remedies - Quiet Title 34:103. Section 34:112 Cancellation of Instruments,</u> deals with Cancellation of Instruments and <u>CCP(California Civil Procedure) Real Property Litigation Chapter 1-8 5:55 V. Quiet Title and Related Actions</u> is where you will look or at least direct your attorney to look for litigating the action. It talks about how the litigation should take place and of course, its very simple and easy to understand. Believe when I say, it's not rocket science, but this subject matter IS very explosive!

Just about every other state in the union has the same type of remedies available to you, all you have to do is look and ask. Take a day and go to the law library in your town or browse the internet and you'll see for yourself! I found it by simply going to the law library and asked the librarian to find it all for me. It took her about nine minutes. Most of the people who work in the Law libraries are extremely helpful, all you have to do is ask.

The wonderful thing about a "quiet title" action is that it is referred to as a friendly lawsuit, because there are no respondents so no one is actually getting sued.

What you are doing is calling is demanding from anyone that might have an interest in your property to present their claim. But let see who or whom that would be? As far as the mortgage on the house is concerned, the originating lender and any subsequent owner of the mortgage down the line from him would be served with papers questioning their validity. The title company that closed the loan might be mentioned as "Trustee." It would be in you loan documents. They could and probably should also be notified. If MERS is in the equation, they also would be notified of an impending action. But let's take a good look at this process in further detail.

By filing of a quiet title action, we're going to be asking the court to cancel any instruments not contested, so if you serve the lender that is actually on title at the county recorders office, you would be serving or notifying the originating lender and Trustee. The service is complete, however, the current investor isn't. Why?

In reality, the investor who currently owns that "note" should be served also, but since there is no assignment to show ownership interest on file, there would be no need to notify them. By not recording all the proper assignments as they should have done and have been done until the system of MERS came around, the lenders using MERS have shot themselves in the foot and are now not required to be notified of this impending action. Therefore, there's no way to defend themselves in this action because they don't even know it's happening since according to public records, they are not the owners of the loan in official record!

Chances are also that some entity like "XYZ Title Company" is listed as trustee on your documents, but if you serve them with papers and you are supposed to do so, because they are listed in recorded documents on title to your property, they would never actually show to contest. Why? There is no reason for them to contest because they don't actually have any right, title or interest to your property! It has absolutely nothing to do with them! But you're covering your bases anyway because that's what the law of Civil Procedure requires. Do you remember what happened to me in the previous chapters with the lack of service on the proper entities? I got my tail handed to me.

When the day comes for the court to hear your case, you will be the only one standing there and the court will generally rule in your favor by "default", which means that you just got a court order to remove all liens from your properties title and now you have a free and clear title to your home which you can market for sale and keep the entire proceeds!

Don't get me wrong! That loan is still out there and you're still responsible for it, but it is now an unsecured obligation on your part just like a credit card debt, which if you choose to do so, you can have eliminated through a bankruptcy petition or just ignore it and let the lender/investor chase you for the balance. Either way, you win! Do you remember what our famous Robert Q. said to me when I asked him why all the struggle and why not just pay me? His answer? Survival! And these days, it seems to be more prevalent than ever!

I believe I should probably reveal to you one of the biggest ironies this country has ever seen, yet few really and truly realize it's magnitude in perspective. As of this writing, January 2011, the "too big to fail banks" just keep getting fatter from dose after dose of government money to keep them solvent while middle America slowly starves. The government has these so-called programs to help homeowners is distress, however, it is the government through Fannie Mae and Freddie Mac that are the largest owners of REO(real estate owned) properties in America. They own approximately seventy five percent of the foreclosed homes being processed for resale in your community. If you don't believe me, pick any foreclosure house listed with your favorite real estate broker and go to the county recorders office and research the title yourself.

Trust me when I say, you will not like what you find. So if you feel guilty about taking an obligation of yours that may or may not belong to one of your favorite lenders and keeping the money for yourself to live and survive in a downward spiraling economy where all your lender has to do is ask Uncle Sam for another handout because you couldn't or didn't pay, then let the chips fall where they may! After all, in the end it's just another credit card you had to borrow against and couldn't pay and nothing more.

The real estate business is the only business I know well and frankly, I don't know how to do anything else. This book was written for you the reader to gain some insight and knowledge in order for you to defend yourself against a sloppy, complacent and faceless machine. The machine has lost it's competitive edge long ago and has become accustomed to getting what it wants when it wants whether right or wrong without question. It is now up to you to make a difference! I've done my part by making you aware of the remedies in place for your benefit. Now it's up to you to get out there and do your part and spread the word to others that need your help, *because now you know how!*

www.ingramcontent.com/pod-product-compliance
Lightning Source LLC
Chambersburg PA
CBHW071454160426
43195CB00013B/2101